A Tribute to James Hillman:
Reflections on a Renegade Psychologist

Edited by Jennifer Leigh Selig
and
Camilo Francisco Ghorayeb

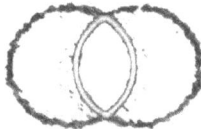

MANDORLA BOOKS

Cover photograph and design by Jennifer Leigh Selig
www.jenniferleighselig.com

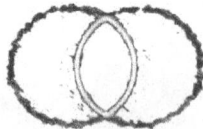

MANDORLA BOOKS
CARPINTERIA, CA
WWW.MANDORLABOOKS.COM

I don't really like the idea of a founder of something
—it's St. Peter on his rock or something—
I think I'd rather be a renegade psychologist.

-James Hillman, from a 2008 interview with Fraser Pierson

TABLE OF CONTENTS

ACKNOWLEDGMENTS

Special thanks to *Cadernos Junguianos* for first publishing the Portuguese edition of this book, and to Camilo Francisco Ghorayeb, Lunalva Fiuza Chagas, Gustavo Barcellos, and others for translating the English lectures into Portuguese.

Special thanks as well to *Quadrant: Journal of the C. G. Jung Foundation* for allowing Safron Rossi and Jennifer Leigh Selig's essays to be reprinted in part and/or whole from the Summer, 2012 edition, XXXXII:2.

EDITORIAL, PORTUGUESE EDITION

A "Tribute to James Hillman" took place on the 15th, 16th, and 17th of March 2013, in Campinas, Brazil. The event was sponsored by Pacifica Graduate Institute of Santa Barbara, California, and by the Universidade Estadual de Campinas, UNICAMP, and was idealized and coordinated by Camilo Francisco Ghorayeb and Lunalva Fiuza Chagas. The aim of the event was to pay homage to the late great North American Jungian analyst and theoretician, deceased in October 2011, and, at the same time, to offer a space for reflection on the impact of his death on our field. The importance of the event and the great interest that the talks immediately provoked on the attending audience, prompted us to prepare a special edition of *Cadernos Junguianos*, the Brazilian Jungian Association's yearly journal, containing the texts of the presentations.

The "Tribute" carried out in Brazil joined other similar events that happened soon after his death in several locations throughout the globe, to remember and celebrate James Hillman and his work. The special collaboration of Pacifica Graduate Institute with the Brazilian event made possible the attendance of several of its teachers and members, experts who dedicate themselves to researching, studying, and teaching Jungian and archetypal psychology. The institution offers Master's and PhD degrees in Depth Psychology (some focusing on community psychology and ecopsychology), Engaged Humanities, and Mythological Studies. Hillman himself was one of the supporters and champions of this now renowned school. He often taught there, and the collection of his archives and manuscripts is kept there, available for research and consultation, together with those of Joseph Campbell, Marija Gimbutas, and Marion Woodman, among others. The Campinas event provided the Brazilian public a meeting with some of these masters (who, incidentally, kept a close relationship with Hillman and his work, and were deeply influenced by him). In addition to that, it was the starting point of a cultural and educational interchange that we deem may bear fruits in the near future.

The texts of this event, reproduced here, show how rich are the reflections of contemporary Jungian debate, and pave the way to the possibility of delving deeper into James Hillman's extraordinary work, and his unique insights. This legacy will forever remain close to a blue fire.

Gustavo Barcellos

TRIBUTE OPENING COMMENTS

Lunalva Fiuza Chagas

James Hillman did not get to the South; he did not step on Brazilian ground.

We had hope. Twice or more we felt his coming, discreet movements, intentions, invitations, and we always expected that Gustavo Barcellos, coordinator of the archetypal psychology study centers in Brazil, would give us the long-awaited news.

However, we slowly received other news. The flesh began to fulfill its destiny, end, pass away. It was a period of grief for us all, especially for me, a double grief, a double goodbye. Via the same ways of the flesh, coincidentally affecting the same organs, my father said goodbye five days before James Hillman.

Unbound from the flesh, his spirit lives on in all of us, proposing new perspectives, transforming the way we perceive, hear, and relate to each other, inching closer with each reading to what is in itself psychological.

James Hillman did not come to Brazil, but sent his colleagues from Pacifica Graduate Institute and his own son to tell us about his unique personality, about the years of work focused on the psyche, marked by his intense and inquisitive nature, born of the relationship of two great forces, Puer and Senex.

That was how in March 2013, certainly a remarkable weekend for all, we received the impressions of those he sent to the South, and we got to know a bit more about the work James Hillman developed in addition to some more intimate information about the man. We could see he was truly tireless in his questioning, determined to move us and remove us from our comfort zone, and doubtlessly, a brilliant man.

Allow me to digress slightly to introduce a few steps towards what we called "A Tribute to James Hillman." Eighteen years ago, I met a man whom I now consider a master of provoking insights, a man who gave me a new appreciation for clinical practice: Gustavo Barcellos. A disciple and friend of James Hillman, he was the pioneer and main force in disseminating archetypal psychology in Brazil, as well as a translator of many works into Brazilian Portuguese.

Throughout all these years Gustavo has not only generously shared his knowledge, but mainly opened for us a new perspective on psychological being, on deepening in our relations with the world, on the psyche itself and the exercise of analysis. Reading archetypal psychology would be difficult and we would be prone to mistakes without a guide, someone already initiated in the mysteries of the imaginal practice, in the nurturing of the soul. Gustavo has taken Hillman's psychology to Brazil's most important centers and continues, now with his own writing, contributing to the field of archetypal psychology in books published in Brazil and the United States.

At the same time, interesting exchanges with Camilo Francisco Ghorayeb pointed to the East. His ability to make connections between martial arts, especially Aikido, and analytical psychology drew my attention. Our regular meetings slowly yet naturally lost their focus on clinical practice and focused more and more on the world and its relations, on Aikido in its own meaning—"the path for unification with the energy of life"—and on mythology and other diverse wonderings.

In one of these meetings, Camilo presented his interests in the low residential study options offered by Pacifica Graduate Institute. We talked at great length, and at our next meeting, as is his nature, he announced he had already scheduled a trip to Pacifica and was about to start coursework for his master's degree. That was a moment of great vitality and movement, one that questioned and disarrayed positions which had been established up until then. Puer itself was crossing the boundaries and uniting North and South, showing the face of the archetype which incites us to walk relentlessly, always seeking and yearning.

Surprisingly, the Tribute came together quickly, with nary a moment to assimilate the deluge of ideas and opportunities. The balancing element amidst this fluidity was, without a doubt, our dear Dr. Jennifer Selig, who saw her vacation in Brazil seven months earlier transform into a lecture journey in Rio de Janeiro, São Paulo, and Campinas. By then I was already involved and contributing as a bridge between North and South. We were greatly supported by the Brazilian Jungian Association (AJB), where I am an Analyst Member, through their Institutes in the cities where the lectures took place. Dr. Jennifer spoke about her latest published work: "The Content of Their Complexes: The Wounded Leadership of Martin Luther King, Jr. and Barack Obama," which was very well received by the public.

I want to take this opportunity to offer gratitude for the support provided by the AJB Institute's personnel: President Dr. Paula Boechat, Dr. Walther Boechat, both Analyst Members of the Rio de Janeiro Institute; Dulce Helena Brizah, President of the São Paulo Institute; Dr. Elisabeth Bauch Zimmerman, President of the Campinas Institute; and Dr. Joel Salles Giglio, Director of Studies at the Institute and our liaison with UNICAMP.

I once again highlight the importance of Dr. Jennifer Selig and her work worthy of a psychopomp, harmonizing acting forces, fostering connections, and bringing out the spiritual character through her involuntary absence at the Tribute. We wish to express our warmth and gratitude to her.

Also with affection I thank the important professors of Pacifica Graduate Institute who have honored us with their participation. I especially thank the founder and current Chancellor of the Institute, Dr. Stephen Aizenstat, and his co-founder and wife Dr. Maren Hansen, for their support, and especially for their fraternal tone towards us. For his special participation, we are also grateful to Laurence Hillman for sharing important and intimate details of the life of his father, our forever beloved James Hillman.

WITHIN IMAGINAL DISTANCE:
TRIBUTE TO JAMES HILLMAN IN BRAZIL

Camilo Francisco Ghorayeb

James Hillman passed away during my first months as a student at Pacifica Graduate Institute, right after the first residential classes of the MA/PhD program in Jungian and Archetypal Studies I had been accepted into, and which emphasized his work. I had had little contact with his ideas at that point, just as I had had little contact with the Jungian community in Brazil. My fascination with having found Pacifica was inevitably mixed with the commotion the whole institute was going through upon his death, for Hillman had been one of the main supporters of the school, together with Joseph Campbell.

The fact that both authors' work formed an important part of the theoretical scaffolding that is taught at Pacifica was decisive in my choosing to study there. My wish was to be closer to whomever had worked and collaborated with them in an attempt to have a more direct experience, absorbing those ideas almost exclusively as an inevitable consequence of such proximity. I felt as if I wanted to go back some steps from a certain "Chinese whisper" that is naturally created until foreign works get as far as Brazil.

It is true that many times we make a point of actually meeting a teacher when we hear that such a one is an authority, such a one carries a type of pioneering spirit or special attitude in one's teachings. We want to see those ideas embodied (really incarnated, within a body) in a human attitude; we are curious about the result, the immediate response with which, as Hillman used to say, that specific living fiction experiences life. Proximity helps teaching, brings ideas to a field of experimentation, modeling, and, although that offers no guarantee of anything, it does seem to make a difference in the development of a personal perception of the phenomenon with which one is getting in touch. The resulting image comes directly out of a concrete exchange, not just an exchange of the imagination, which is what we create as an alternative to understand or introject when no access to the authority is possible. The people, the places where we are, the smells, the colors, the specific movements, they all build unique impressions.

This could easily be misunderstood as idealization and even adoration, but at the end of the day it appears to be true that travelling to Mecca at least once in your life does not only serve your faith, but also provides the opportunity to imagine it from a different perspective, an embodied perspective. When I thought of Brazil, and of the great distance to other worlds that Brazilians have learned to see as part of Brazilianhood (which, perhaps, dates back to the birth of the country, when a fictional story about a bastard condition began to be told and retold), my wish was to be closer, to reduce the distance between myself and the other world that Pacifica represented.

We Brazilians have lived with such distance for far too many years. As a teenager who grew up in São Paulo listening to many great contemporary rock bands, I remember hearing numerous times that I would have to wait until all my favorite bands got to the end of their careers to see them play live. It seems Brazil was barely ever included in any international tour happening in the world, and artists only decided to come here when no other place seemed interesting anymore.

Whether this is true or not, this oft-repeated story reveals a lot about the fictions that permeated this country's psyche. It is true that much has changed; Brazil has become much more visible to the world in many ways and, indeed, it appears the distance has been reduced. But the fact is that the changes that are beginning to move this country away from an isolated condition are challenged by own deep historical entrenchment, and the daunting task of reverting stigmas that we have both introjected and internally multiplied, reproducing the same result. And there is also the distance projected onto Brazil, as shown by psychologist Gustavo Barcellos in his article "South and Archetypal Psychology: The Brazilian Experience," presented in an Archetypal Psychology conference held in California in the year 2000. According to Gustavo, the South of archetypal psychology is not as south as it could be or as Brazil is. The ocean that separates us from the north seems to be a mythical bordering locus of oblivion, just as it was in Brazil's birth into the world, when those who arrived here behaved in dissonant ways compared to the moral rules they followed back in the north, for they considered no sin existed below the Equator.

This was one of the narratives within which Brazil grew, and which Brazilians inherited in different versions—that we were far away from the Northern world, that we were not being imagined by this world and not imagining ourselves within this world. The distance is, in fact, concrete—Brazil is a huge country, continental, alone in its own language (Portuguese) in America—but it also appears to be more imaginal, more of a narrative essence, a perception or perhaps misperception that Brazilians took as sheer truth. Hence the well-known extreme reactions to foreign visitors, where we either treat them with careless disdain as if they were still conquerors or exploiters, or with an excessive idealization and submission as if they fulfilled prophecies of long-awaited saviors. Such imaginings are, apparently, still quite alive and active in the country's psyche. And whereas one may argue that the heroic journeys of a few isolated individuals who have managed to cross that imaginal abyss, reaching international visibility (Brazilians who have literally become heroes in the country for having struggled and succeeded completely on their own, such as Gustavo Kuerten in tennis, and Ayton Senna in Formula One racing) may have offered a way out to the whole nation, one must not forget that the same heroes also carry and expose the proof of Brazil's psychic distance. Imaginal distance, much as it happens with any psychic material, needs to be traversed within, in order to allow us to express our identity and offer ourselves to the world, becoming, as a result, part of it, and avoiding extremisms. But also in the same way as it happens with the individual psyche, Brazil will only be able to turn to itself, to its own psychic discomforts, through the eyes of the different other, in its relationship with the concrete and imaginal foreign world. Then, the proximity with the world becomes the proximity within ourselves.

These perceptions about my country became vivid to me as I visited Pacifica Graduate Institute in the foreign land of North America, which itself was loaded with the foreign commotion of such an important loss in the passing of James Hillman, and they led me eventually to ask the chair of my program at Pacifica, Dr. Jennifer Selig, about the possibility of having a tribute to Hillman in Brazil along the lines of the one I had seen at Pacifica in late winter following his death. The fact that I didn't hear any discouragements bothered my own imaginal distance. Could it be that it was that easy to start a relationship between Brazil and Pacifica, between South and North?

Back home I took the idea to the only person in the Jungian community at that time with whom I was in contact: Lunalva Chagas. Again, not one discouraging word, not even a suggestion that it was much too big an event (and it was) to be put together. Much to the contrary, Lunalva was thrilled and excited by such an idea. She had a long list of contacts, and as soon as she heard about Dr. Selig's upcoming trip to Brazil to explore possible venues and partners for actualizing a southern "Tribute to James Hillman," she parlayed that visit into four lectures given by Jennifer in three different cities: Rio de Janeiro, São Paulo, and Campinas.

The feeling during the time of those lectures was that of an embryonic tribute quickening into a viable life, as things began to happen by themselves. We lost the only venue I knew of where we could hold the event, when all of a sudden, shortly after Dr. Selig's talk in Campinas, Dr. Joel Giglio with his habitual enthusiasm invited us to go to the University of Campinas (UNICAMP), where he taught a course on Jungian psychology. After no more than one meeting, the location problem was solved—the homage would be paid in the second best university in Brazil. I began to work on organizing and advertising the event, following the original idea of having three professors from Pacifica offering lectures, in addition to the presence of Gustavo Barcellos, Dr. Hillman's official translator from English to Portuguese, the one responsible for disseminating Dr. Hillman's work in Brazil. But one night in my apartment in Campinas, we began to dream bigger, and Dr. Selig thought of other important guests who could join us; she sent out emails to many of them that very night, and we received enthusiastic confirmations almost immediately. We were deeply thrilled. Our tribute had grown from four to nine guests, including Dr. Hillman's wife, Margot McLean, who would present a video of her husband in his last moments, a work the couple had produced and which had only been shown before in a memorial tribute in New York City.

The tribute, however, continued to suffer sudden changes we could not expect, constantly reminding us that it was truly alive and had a will of its own. Margot McLean was the first to cancel. Close to the final stretch both Dr. Selig and Dr. Glen Slater faced challenges and, with deep sorrow, could not make it to the tribute (fortunately, they both took part in the tribute through this book, offering us for publication the same texts which they had planned to read at the time). For Dr. Selig, debilitating issues with her back caused her to be unable to fly, and I bore witness to how devastated she became after learning she could not come to the tribute to which she had contributed so much (and which was honoring a beloved teacher of hers, as she writes about in her essay in this volume). I carried her badge with me during the whole event in an attempt to have at least a little bit of her present. On the other hand, Laurence Hillman, James Hillman's son, promptly accepted Margot McLean's invitation to come in her stead, and Dr. Safron Rossi, Curator of Collections at OPUS Archives and Research Center (the center located onsite at Pacifica which preserves, among other important scholars, James Hillman's and Joseph Campbell's archives and manuscripts) agreed to speak about her contact with Hillman during the three last years of his life, when she helped him organize all the work he kept in his house, from his manuscripts to unpublished talks, lectures, letters, and more.

So much turbulence, normal to the eyes of anyone who has put together an event of this kind, seemed quite despairing to me, as I was going through it for the first time. But the whole situation also defied that heroic image I created for myself, thinking I had covered that imaginal distance. I came to see that a hero should not come forth as a solution, as someone who is bound to grab destiny with his own hands. The tribute, shaping up by itself, deconstructed the heroic ego arising out of the need to overcome belief in the distance, just as it helped me work through some of my own personal issues and cultural perceptions. Rather than hunting for myself and my culture throughout the world, I learned that I (and we) can stay in our homeland and earn the presence I (and we) already have but do not recognize.

Now, with the tribute in the past, connections between North and South seem stronger and it is my wish that they continue to become so. It is also my wish that Pacifica may come more often to Brazil and, eventually "Brazilianize" itself, opening up a way for Brazil to go to California so that our country, remembered as a present part of the world, rather than forgotten, may contribute to Pacifica's own mission, one of "tending the soul of the world," an image which was warmly fostered by James Hillman's archetypal psychology.

I extend my sincere thanks to everyone who took part in the "Tribute to James Hillman" and helped to reduce the literal and imaginal distance. I would especially like to thank Dr. Jennifer Selig, Lunalva Chagas, and Gustavo Barcellos for betting on this idea with all their support—along with the Board of the Jungian Association of Brazil (AJB)—and for helping publish the Tribute talks in Portuguese. Special thanks also go to Dr. Joel Giglio for his spontaneous and important collaboration all the way, and to all the professors from Pacifica Graduate Institute who agreed to participate without hesitation. Last, my warmest thanks to Pacifica's Chancellor and founder Dr. Stephen Aizenstat and his wife, Pacifica's co-founder Dr. Maren Hansen, for the ever-growing involvement, acknowledgment, and belief in this relationship—which sometimes offers uncomfortable and challenging situations—and for always keeping it ethical and transparent, a greatly important example, if not the greatest, which can be brought to our country.

References

Barcellos, G. (2000). South and archetypal psychology: The Brazilian experience. In D. P. Slattery, & L. Corbett (Eds.), *Psychology at the threshold* (pp. 243-259). Carpinteria, CA: Pacifica Graduate Institute Publications.

HONORING JAMES HILLMAN

Stephen Aizenstat

It is good to be here with you in Brazil to honor James Hillman. James was one of my dearest friends and a cherished mentor when Pacifica Graduate Institute was dreamed into being nearly 40 years ago. Pacifica's motto, *anima mundi colendae gratia*—for the sake of tending soul in the world—was partly inspired by Hillman's passion for the soul in and of the world. As we all know, James cared deeply for the *anima mundi* and believed that a psychology that pays attention only to the inner life of people was inadequate. As early as 1972 he noticed that "we flee the sickness of the contemporary world into analysis" (p. 4). A few years later, in *Re-Visioning Psychology*, James named this the "personalistic fallacy," which we commit every time we "speak of my anima and my soul" (1975, p. 49). He confessed that he was "astounded by life and beauty in the patients vis-a-vis the dead and ugly world they inhabit" (1992, p. 92) He realized that "the self-knowledge that depth psychology offers is not enough if the depths of the world soul are neglected" (1985, p. 108).

James returned to this theme—the inadequacy of a psychology that ignores the *anima mundi*—again and again, perhaps with the greatest passion in his 1982 essay "*Anima Mundi*: The Return of the Soul to the World." There, he urged us to deepen our imagination of the world. "Not only animals and plants ensouled as in the Romantic vision, but soul is given with each thing. God-given things of nature and man-made things of the street" (p. 77). To honor the passion James

15

felt for the soul of the world in each and every thing, natural and man-made, I am orienting this talk around three ideas. First, that the organicity and intelligence of dreamspace is being threatened by the omnipresence of cyberspace; second, that the exponential expansion of cyberspace dissolves thresholds of privacy and results in severe physiological and psychological afflictions particularly for our youth; and third, in this time of immediate planetary peril, the tools offered by cyberspace, and in particular by social networking, may allow us to listen into the world's dream in ways as yet imagined. So let's begin.

When our eyes close, something else comes awake. We cross a threshold into another landscape, apart from the persons and things of ordinary waking reality. The solar brightness of the day, extended through artificial lighting as the sun goes down, gives way to darkness as the world behind the visible world presents itself. With closed eyes comes sleep and dream, perhaps the most endangered domain in our hyperactive, hyper-connected contemporary world. It is here, in the dreamtime, that the others who go unnoticed and unwelcomed in light of the day reveal their presence, offer their voice, and remind us of their place in the circle of life. Perhaps the real "tragedy of the commons" in today's world is the loss of lyrical dream space to a ubiquitous and agitated cyberspace. More dangerous than the depletion of precious natural resources is the depletion of sleep, and, thus, dream, by a manic culture that sees no value in rest. Instead, it seems hell-bent on propping open the last remaining threshold between worlds—our eyelids—in some Clockwork Orange nightmare, foreclosing access to a vast, intelligent, and yet-to-be-explored sanctuary: the dreamtime.

Eyelids, so simple in anatomy, so profound in effect. They are as literal as a blink, as metaphoric as the river Styx, that mythic boundary between ego consciousness and the underworld of sleep and dream that "gives absolute order to the Gods themselves," Hillman tells us (1979, p. 59). Eyes open illuminates the wonders and the horrors of the outer world, the physical real. Eyes closed "lets the sweet surrender of sleep befall" and gives place to the figures of the inner world of memory and imagination. With eyelids closed, we open to the limitless capacity of the deep soul, the world behind the world. Yet paradoxically, with our eyelids open, we also can perceive the deep soulfulness in the world, the subtle beauty of the landscapes we walk through each and every day. All that is required is attention which James considered "the cardinal psychological virtue" because it is essential to the practice of any of the other cardinal virtues. As he tells us in his book *Insearch*, "There can hardly be faith nor hope nor love for anything unless it first receives attention" (1994, p. 119).

The Endangered World of the Dream

Yet the world of the dream is endangered. Multiple research studies conducted over several decades report that people today are getting by with less and less sleep as we live more complicated, accelerated lives. The computer and Internet technologies that we once thought would grant us more leisure have instead proved overwhelming and exhausting. "In less than the span of a single childhood, Americans have merged with their machines," reports an August 2012 *Newsweek* essay. We are "staring at a screen for at least eight hours a day, more time than we spend on any other activity including sleeping. . . . Web use often displaces sleep, exercise, and face-to-face exchanges." Some smartphone users "check their phones before bed, in the middle of the night, if they stir, and within minutes of waking up. . . . [because] every ping could be a social, sexual, or professional opportunity" (Dokoupil, 2012, pp. 27-29).

The ongoing assault of information is more pervasive, more intense, and more threatening than at any time in human history. As Sherry Turkle from MIT puts it, "We are all cyborgs now" (2012, p. 152).

Online, we easily find "company" but are exhausted by the pressures of performance. We enjoy continual connection but rarely have each other's full attention. We can have instant audiences but flatten out what we say to each other in new reductive genres of abbreviation. . . . We can work from home, but our work bleeds into our private lives until we can barely discern the boundaries between them. We like being able to reach each other almost instantaneously but have to hide our phones to force ourselves to take a quiet moment. (p. 280)

If we are consumed by screen time of every shape and form, always on, always connected, how often will we make the time to receive the radiance of the *anima mundi*? If we sacrifice sleep in order to stay connected, how will we have the time to dream?

This well-spring of human imagination, the world behind the world, where the ancestors live—and what our elders die into—is endangered now. The homeland, where dream figures are birthed, struggles now and is in peril. Yes, that place, the transcendent dimension of consciousness, the dreamtime, the terrain of the invisibles, the realm of "soul-making" where the wisdom stories of the collective, even the world unconscious reside, is threatened by the encroachment of something other.

This other is the Internet, or cyberspace, a dynamic, revolutionary, even some would say evolutionary technology. Brilliant in design, versatile, and powerful, with thousands of apps added each year, the web offers us unprecedented opportunity to dissolve space and connect with others. Yet this connective tissue is electronic, not organic, and it threatens to overtake or, at minimum, invade the living psyche in two ways. First, by luring us into the online world, many of us sacrifice sleep and the dreamtime. Second, the voices originating from the indigenous psyche are being increasingly muted, silenced. Like shopping malls constructed on top of natural landscapes, so too the *genius loci*, or "spirit of place," is experiencing the intrusion of a new conquering technological civilization with a mind and voice of its own.[1]

---

[1] The classical scholar Elizabeth Vandiver notes in *Classical Mythology* (2001) that of the four key differences between the Greek world and contemporary civilization, the one most remote and strange to moderns is polytheism. The dozens of named gods known throughout the entire culture were enhanced by hundreds of local "place" gods, spirit, or daimons. These *genius loci* rendered Greek polytheism into a persistent, embodied, living experience. It was not just that there were many gods: the entire world

When cyberspace mutes the particular voices of the *genius loci*, it reduces our sensitivity to what Hillman calls "the natural polytheism of the psyche" (1975, p. 127). Imaginal intelligence gives way to information intelligence. The authentic images rooted in the deep psyche are replaced by counterfeit images, collections of pixels that are designed to sell products, create profit, and promote agendas of every kind. With all of its fantastic accomplishments, from Mapquest to Google search, from dating services to online shopping, from military surveillance to drone missile targeting, from applied robot applications to automated computer graphics, cyberspace must not replace the timeless textural phenomenology of the dreamscape or the aliveness of embodied experience. When the threshold between the two blurs, the genius alive in the natural psyche of persons and places grows dim.

Cyberculture and the Erosion of Place

The kind of digital power that once required an entire room full of equipment now fits nicely in the palm of your hand or comfortably on your lap. Such sleek, compact devices are portals to clouds full of digital information. There is never a need to be without the Internet and, for some, an ever-present need to connect. It's estimated that one-third of smartphone users go online before getting out of bed (Dokoupil, 2012, p. 28).

In fact, there are some people who will not give up their digital devices, even for one day, even as part of a research project. A study conducted by the University of Maryland asked 200 undergraduates to forgo the use of smartphones, tablets, and laptops for one day and keep a journal of their feelings. Two other universities, seeking to duplicate the research, have been unable to find enough volunteers to conduct the study. "Most college students are not just unwilling, but functionally unable, to be without their media links to the world" (Dokoupil, 2012, p. 28). The University of Maryland study and other

---

and all the things in it was alive and sacred, feeling and speaking. This is precisely what Hillman challenged us to remember.

research "is now making it clear that the Internet is not 'just' another delivery system. It is creating a whole new mental environment, a digital state of nature where the human mind becomes a spinning instrument panel, and few people will survive unscathed" (p. 27).

If the human mind has become a flashing instrument panel, then mental acuity is the way in to this digital world. To roam the territory, master the games, work the sophisticated software, cerebral dexterity is cultivated. Children, outfitted with cell phones and tablet computers by the age of three or four, already navigate this digital world at warp speed. And, there can be little doubt that once they cross the threshold, lured by the limitless possibility of cyberspace, they enter a virtual landscape, an electronic ecosystem, that knows no boundaries of time or place.

Possibly one of the most interesting examples of the lure of the virtual landscape is an online social matrix known as Second Life. When someone joins Second Life the first task is to create a virtual self, an avatar. Then the avatar, the virtual "you," hangs out "in virtual bars, restaurants, and cafes. You relax on virtual beaches and have business meetings in virtual conference rooms" (Turkle, 2012, p. 158). Some Second Lifers, dissatisfied in the physical real, compensate through creative encounters in the digital real.

Another place in which people of all ages, but especially adolescents, inhabit a cyberworld is through online gaming. Role-playing games are as old as humanity. What is new is where these games take place and how much of the body is actually present. First generation online games typically featured a quest motif, offering a fantasy of action and adventure, the opportunity to be a hero. Today's games are far more elaborate, such as the massively multi-player online role-playing games, "MMORGs" for short, that tweens, teens, and some adults play for hours, even days, at a time. *World of Warcraft*, the most popular, lets users play in the digital world of Azeroth, along with nearly 12 million other gamers around the world.

> There, you control a character, an avatar, whose personality, natural gifts, and acquired skills are under continual

> development as it takes on a trade, explores the landscape, fights monsters, and goes on quests. In some games, you can play alone—in which case you mostly have artificial intelligences for company, "bots" that play the role of human characters. Or you can band together with other players on the network to conquer new worlds. (Turkle, 2012, p. 158)

Such games are not only their own world, they can become the gamer's entire world, "a social life unto itself: you routinely email, talk to, and message the people you game with" (Turkle, 2012, p. 158).

Thus in the world of the digital real—to distinguish it from the physical real—place takes on some very strange meanings. If each device we use is a portal to another world and if, on a single device such as the average desktop computer, we can open multiple windows each one a portal to another world, how can we say where we are at any one time? *Where is there?* And are we really *there* if our attention is fractured into multiple competing environments, conversations, and tasks? These questions have propelled passionate debate among psychologists over formalizing "Internet addiction disorder" (IAD) by installing it in the 5th edition of the *Diagnostic and Statistical Manual of Mental Disorders* (DSM-V). Supporters argue that addiction to the Internet is proliferating:

> In the past, people reported to have an Internet addiction disorder were stereotyped as young, introverted, socially awkward, computer-oriented males. While this stereotype may have been true in the past, the availability of computers and the increased ease of access to the Internet are quickly challenging this notion. As a result, problematic Internet use can be found worldwide in any age group, social class, racial or ethnic group, level of education and income, and gender. One researcher in the Boston area estimates that between 6% and 10% of people who surf the Web suffer from some type of Internet dependency; and the American Academy of Pediatrics (AAP) estimates that between 8% and 12% of American children and

adolescents have IAD. (Beard & Frey, 2012, "Demographics," ¶1)

Those opposing the idea argue that IAD is not a distinctive disorder but "simply an instance of a new technology being used to support other addictions" (Beard & Frey, 2012, "Definitions," ¶2). This debate will no doubt continue, but almost no one questions the reach of digital technology and the powerful influence of cyberspace on human life. With fewer tangible, meaningful borders, less focused human interaction, and very little sleep, we are a people captivated, and depleted, by the screen.

Cyberculture and the Erosion of the Senses

There are real consequences of cyber-consumption, both for our generation and, in addition to those who will follow. As participants in this limitless labyrinth, we lose contact with body, with our personal animal body, our senses. As participants in this limitless labyrinth, we lose contact with "the soft animal" of our body—to borrow Mary Oliver's lovely phrase (1992, p. 110). We also lose sensuous contact with the body of the world as it presents itself in the sharp needles of a fragrant pine tree, the musty scent of sage warmed by the afternoon sun, and the feel of oozy mud along a riverbank. Can you smell an email, can you taste a text message, or can you feel the texture of an e-book? Captured in a galaxy of images, words, and numbers displayed on screens of every shape and size and allure, we become ever more isolated from our animal body and from those of others who we interact with in embodied relationships. We need occasional "shelter from the storm" of screen time, or else we will pay the price. *For many, crossing the threshold into cyber-technology splits us from the core of our Being, the source of life, animated by the psyche of Nature.* We lose authentic relationship with ourselves and with others, our experience of belonging. We need sustained contact with the core of our being rather than over-dependence on the mind of the machine. Over-determined by who meets us on screen, we get lonely.

Connected and Lonely

John Cacioppo, the director of the Center for Cognitive and Social Neuroscience at the University of Chicago, is one of the world's leading experts on loneliness. In Stephen Marche's 2012 essay "Is Facebook Making Us Lonely?" he cites some of Cacioppo's research proving "when you are lonely, your whole body is lonely" (Marche, 2012, ¶25). And, not surprisingly, "being lonely is extremely bad for your health. You're more likely to be obese, less likely to exercise, to survive a serious operation, more likely to be depressed, to sleep badly and to suffer dementia and general cognitive decline" (¶13).

The promise of the phrase "global village" is the warmth and reassurance of community, sustained by the ordinary, day-to-day meetings, spontaneous, casual, heartfelt, that constitute so much of a well-balanced life. The Internet seemed to promise that anyone, nearly anywhere on the planet could become our neighbor, and wouldn't that alleviate some of our loneliness? In fact, wouldn't the digital world, available 24/7, offer even more social contact since ordinary considerations like time zone and geographical place no longer matter? Cacippo's research looked for a connection between the loneliness of the participants in his study and the amount of time they used social media in the digital real, including Facebook, online games, chat rooms, and dating services. The results were unequivocal. "The greater the proposition of face-to-face interactions the less lonely you are, the more you are in virtual reality, the lonelier you become" (as quoted in Marche, 2012, ¶27). The Internet, used as a tool to generate more direct interaction, is one thing. Yet the fact remains that Facebook, with over one trillion page views in a month, and an average of over three billion "likes" and comments every day, is interfering with our real friendships, distancing us from each other. Social networking, by dissolving time and place, which are the boundaries needed for friendship in the physical real, might be spreading the very isolation it seemed designed to conquer.

Leading stories in American media just in the last few months have focused on this topic. The digital world is clearly not as warm, reassuring, or sustaining as some hoped. The cover essay of *The Atlantic*, "Is Facebook Making us Lonely?" is accompanied by a haunting photograph of a nude couple, embracing. She rests her head on his shoulder, both arms encircling him, eyes gently closed. He holds her with one arm while staring at the mesmerizing glow of a digital device gripped in his other hand. The picture says it all, but Marche's essay is well worth reading. He says that for many of us, our web of connections—those made possible by the Internet and those that occur without it, in the day-to-day physical real—has grown broader but shallower:

> We are living in an isolation that would have been unimaginable to our ancestors, and yet we have never been more accessible. Over the past three decades, technology has delivered to us a world in which we need not be out of contact for a fraction of a moment. . . . Yet within this world of instant and absolute communication, unbounded by limits of time or space, we suffer from unprecedented alienation. We have never been more detached from one another, or lonelier. In a world consumed by ever more novel modes of socializing, we have less and less actual society. We live in an accelerating contradiction: the more connected we become, the lonelier we are. (Marche, 2012, pp. 60-62)

Marche concludes with this frightening statement: "We were promised a global village; instead we inhabit the drab cul-de-sacs and endless freeways of a vast suburb of information" (2012, p. 62).

The Disappearance of Recollection and Reflection

There are additional consequences of losing contact with the natural psyche and to the privacy of our interiority. Getting caught in the maze of cyberspace subjects us, ever more so, to symptoms of fear, paranoia, and reactive behaviors. In contemporary culture, we all feel the constant worry of being exposed, caught in a lie, subjected to a mischaracterization, a gesture taken the wrong way. Our natural fears escalate when time in the manic information age is measured in milliseconds and not days. Then, there is little effort or space to contain, reflect, and reconsider—mere seconds pass before we react impulsively to what anybody says or does. This too, says Turkle, is part of cyberculture and in particular the advent of social media:

> Online, social networks instruct us to share whenever there's "something on our mind," no matter how ignorant or ill considered, and then help us broadcast it to the widest possible audience. Every day each of us is bombarded by other people's random thoughts. (Turkle, 2012, p. 276)

Thoughtlessness in cyberculture is viral: instant transmission, global dissemination.

Remember, when we would think about "the cycle of life," rooted in the rhythms of the natural world? No longer is this the case; Nature's "cycle" is now Technologies' "tweet." Or worse, a post on Facebook, or YouTube, gone viral, ends up on the 24/7 newsflash, repeated over and again, on one or more of the over 2000 television networks news broadcasts, or tens of thousands Internet Broadcast Networks. Instant communication brings with it a culture of increased fear, paranoia, and hyperactive vigilance. Thresholds of time, like the day ending with the night falling and the morning newspaper coming with the dawn's early light, is a relic of another time, another era.

Digital Bullies

The speed of digital communication does not reward the slow time needed to reflect and assess. It rewards haste and thoughtlessness. Now, anyone can launch an instantaneous attack on another person from the disembodied anonymity of a laptop, tablet, or smartphone. With the ease of a few keyboard strokes, they can take aim at anyone, at any time, and anywhere. Commentary, or what some have named "free speech," is less a matter of conscious reflection with consequences and more an expression of unmediated cathartic rage. In fact, there is even an ethical rationale and a psychological justification ascribed to such behavior. The power and usefulness of the Internet, designed for "the people," depends on zero censorship. The perpetrator, it can be argued, acts in a "therapeutic way" that is condoned as being direct, not holding back, or being up front. There is little accountability for such intrusive messaging and no protection from the next barrage, whether factual or fabricated. It is in this "no holds barred" environment that some of the most brutal damage is done, particularly to young people.

Bullying, long a feature of the schoolyard, takes on new intensity in the world of cyberspace. Teachers report that classroom interaction does not end when the school day is over but continues the moment the last period ends and well into the wee hours of the night. Just years ago students went home for some well needed respite, some down time—to recover, renew, and regenerate. All of this has changed in the years since Facebook, chat rooms, websites, and texting. Social chatter is constant, in class and out. It never stops, never winds down. Gossip has a life of its own, sometimes taking on a self-generating momentum that spins out of control, fueled by envy, a grudge, or simple stupidity. In all instances, the attack creates havoc. Mean group text messaging, rumors posted on social media sites, embarrassing pictures, videos, or fake profiles, create social pressures that easily find a scapegoat, a defenseless target. No longer experienced as a real person, the student is reduced to a cyber-target.

Teachers report, over and again, that kids who have been targeted come to school the next day, dazed, demolished, socially and psychologically devastated. They have been subjected to peer ridicule, false accusations, threatening messages, and sexting, the circulation of sexually suggestive pictures or messages. Their identities are stolen and then used to send nasty, embarrassing messages that damage even the strongest friendships. All of this occurs after-hours, in cyberspace, where it is split off from any kind of embodied relational contact. There are no borders, no privacy, and no downtime for the victims, and certainly little opportunity for defense. Once texts or images are circulated on the Internet, they may resurface again and again. In cyberspace, almost nothing is deleted completely. Any notion of a genuine personal sanctuary is now a relic of the past.

Several organizations compile information about cyberbullying including the i-SAFE Foundation and the Cyberbullying Research Center. The picture that emerges is truly frightening.

- Over half of adolescents have been bullied online, and about the same number have engaged in cyberbullying.
- More than one in three young people have experienced cyberthreats online.
- One in 10 adolescents or teens have had embarrassing or damaging pictures taken of themselves without their permission, often using cell phone cameras.
- Cyberbullying affects both sexes and all races, and the victims are more likely to have low self-esteem and to consider suicide.
- Well over half of young people do not tell their parents when cyberbullying occurs.

Fox Visits Now

I would like to conclude my remarks with a personal story, a story many of you may, in your own way, recognize. It is a true account of crossing the threshold into another time and space. To close, I will offer how this tale of traversing the divide informs what is possible going forward; how, in fact, when used differently, the exceptional capacities of cyber-scape provide the tools to harvest the intelligence rooted in the psyche of the dream-scape. I will take a few moments to describe what we are developing at Pacifica Graduate Institute: The Global Dream Initiative.

My day job comes to its final closing. Not at 5 p.m. as intended and planned, but, sustained by my adrenalin, pushed by my desire, and caught in my addiction to completion—the hand of the clock now sweeps well past 7:30. Ouch. What happened? Too much to do, new information flooding in, a stream of new emails and texts appearing on my tablet and smartphone every few minutes, from time zones whose clocks show different numbers than the one displayed on my computer or on the face ticking forward on the wall above my desk. Yep, the world never sleeps, always in continuous activity. Night and day merge in the global matrix of timeless motion. The rapids of information-overload break through the sturdiest of dams that I construct to make sure that, this time, I get the hell out of here, before sunset. Yet, here we go again, new data, questions, demands, all rushing through those "borders" intended to keep the flooding torrents of information at bay. The interior lowlands of psyche, my place of sanctuary, are once again, underwater. Longing to salvage some leisure time on the dry island above the deluge, exhaustion finally sets in, agonizingly so, and it's time to go home.

Overextended, again, something out of the ordinary happens. Driving home from work, following the same route I have taken for 20 years, I am surprised. Through the urban maze of asphalt roads slanting underneath two concrete bridges designed for the interstate, I notice something I have never seen before. A sleek, richly colored red tail fox walks mindfully and patiently across the road, one step at a time. In awe, I notice, stopping my vehicle on the spot. Parked in the middle of the street, cars lining up behind or swerving around, drivers waste no time speeding by, determined to arrive at their particular destination on time. Yet, enraptured by the beauty and majesty of Fox, something different was happening for me. Wonder had come into my life, as Fox and I entered a different quality of time and place. Crossing the threshold of the familiar, I paused and lingered. We gazed at each other, and the world became a bigger place. The traffic became background, the noise and the bridges and roads gave way to something other. The landscape changed. Fox, so sleek in form, shimmering in red and brown with a big bushy tail, matching the full length of its upper body, paused and took me in, as I did Fox. The separation between the human-constructed and nature-given dissolved into another, more unified, way of being. We shared a different kind of time, the intimacy of "private time." Like in a dream, Fox visited, and stayed for what seemed an eternity. Now walking slowly in the patch of land between the freeway and the overpass, Fox was looking back at me time and again, inviting me into a realm beyond the ordinary. I felt blessed, an invitation to remember . . . to re-experience how quickly the threshold dividing the over-habituated, machine-conditioned, urban-programed, can dissolve and surrender to an animated realm alive with the visitants of Nature's dream. As Fox visits now, everything slowed down. In the aesthetic of full display, Fox opened me into an ancient way of knowing, one animal body to another. An echo of remembrance, alive, on the other side of the divide sounded and I felt a sense of deep belonging, a homecoming, to that which sources us both. Over the threshold, the world behind the world, an enchanted, ensouled, embodied world offered herself—without a screen—to my imagination.

A Global Dream Initiative

Here, in this extended field of imagination, I recall the words of James Hillman. "Let us imagine the *anima mundi* as that particular soul-spark, that seminal image, which offers itself through each thing in its visible form" (1982, p. 77). We know that the idea of an ensouled or animated world is a natural part of many indigenous traditions: James did not invent it. But he did remind us that the *anima mundi* has no home in much of contemporary culture. Instead, we have acted as though soul exists inside ourselves, inside our moods and feelings, inside our personal dreams and relationships. We have acted as though soul sickness has nothing whatsoever to do with the landscapes in which we live and work and play.

"The archetypal source of our world's continuing peril," Hillman tells us, is "the fateful neglect, the repression, of the *anima mundi*" (1982, p. xx). Today, we can honor James by remembering the suffering of the *anima mundi*, the ensouled world. We can serve as witnesses to the many ways in which the world is becoming conscious of itself through that suffering, as he pointed out.

But we choose to address the world's suffering though something we are calling the Global Dream Initiative. This initiative, which crucially depends on Internet technology, honors Hillman's vision of the *anima mundi* as "that particular soul-spark, that seminal image, which offers itself through each thing in its visible form" (1982, p. x). When all things, *both natural and man-made,* have soul and their presence has psychic reality, then we can imagine the fruitful and life-enhancing possibilities inherent in cyberspace which can and must be set alongside its invasive, destructive potential.

We propose to combine the dreaming of the world—the intelligence of psyche in all being—with the capacity to harvest and disseminate these dreams through the tools of social networking. The original creative promise of a worldwide web of connected and impassioned individuals can, through a Global Dream Initiative, foster communities of dreamers from all over the globe who witness the world's suffering in the dreamtime. What is being asked of us now is not what we can do to save the planet, but, rather, what is the planet, through her dreams, asking of us now?

To hear the dreams of the world present their intelligence through the dream images of people worldwide, necessitates the use of cyber-technology. Here, we discover the new, a threshold that encourages the depth of privacy and dream in conjunction with the breadth of social networking and Internet communication. At Pacifica, through cyber-technology we will:

- Offer an animated web-based education in an imaginal approach to world suffering. The aim will be to inspire people to adopt the ancient notion of the *anima mundi*—a world alive and full of soul in everyone and every thing, whether natural or manufactured.
- Gather dreams and dreamers. We will ask for dreams and, using software technology for grouping them, offer them back

to the dreamers, grouped by image or theme, thus forming a kind of dream-centered tribal affiliation across borders on a global scale.

- Use web-based communication as a tool for interacting with the "pattern that connects" to allow the autonomy of the dreaming psyche to reveal herself in service of the world's soul.

Closing

All of us, since the relationship with the Internet began, have tended to accept it as it is, without much conscious thought about how we want it to be or what we want to avoid. Those days of complacency should end. The Internet is still ours to shape. Our minds are in the balance. (Dokoupil, 2012, p. 30)

We stand at a critical moment in earth's history. Humanity is part of a vast, evolving universe. The forces of nature make existence a demanding and uncertain adventure, but earth has provided the conditions essential to life's evolution. The global environment with its finite resources is a common concern of all peoples. The protection of Earth's vitality, diversity, and beauty is a sacred trust. In memory of James, and in tribute to his call to tend the soul of the world, let us all join in that sacred trust and let psyche speak to us, and through us, in her many voices so that the world in all its fruitful diversity endures.

References

Beard, K. & Frey, R. (2012). Internet addiction disorder. In K. Key (Ed.), *The Gale Encyclopedia of Mental Health* (3rd ed., Vol. 1, pp. 829-833). Detroit, MI: Gale. Retrieved from http://go.galegroup.com/ps/i.do?id=
GALE%7CCX4013200247&v=2.1&u=carp39441&it=r&p=GVR

L&sw=w

Dokoupil, T. (2012). Tweets. Texts. Emails. Posts. Is the onslaught making us crazy? *Newsweek*, July 16, 2012, 24-30.

Hillman, J. (1972). *The myth of analysis: Three essays in archetypal psychology*. Evanston, IL: Northwestern University Press.

Hillman, J. (1975). *Re-visioning psychology*. New York, NY: Harper & Row.

Hillman, J. (1979). *The dream and the underworld*. New York, NY: Harper & Row.

Hillman, J. (1982). *Anima mundi*: The return of the soul to the world. *Spring 1982*, 71-93. Dallas, TX: Spring Publications.

Hillman, J. (1985). *Anima: Anatomy of a personified notion*. Dallas, TX: Spring Publications.

Hillman, J. (1992). *The thought of the heart and the soul of the world*. Dallas, TX: Spring Publications.

Hillman, J. (1994). *Insearch: Psychology and religion*. Woodstock, CT: Spring Publications.

Marche, S. (2012). Is Facebook making us lonely? *The Atlantic*, May 2012, 59-65.

Oliver, M. (1992). *New and selected poems*. Boston, MA: Beacon Press.

Rosin, H. (2013). The touch-screen generation. *The Atlantic*, April 2013, 56-65.

Turkle, S. (2012). *Alone together: Why we expect more from technology and less from each other*. New York, NY: Basic Books.

Vandiver, E. (2001). *Classical mythology*. Chantilly, VA: The Teaching Company.

SLIGHTLY AT ODDS:
JAMES HILLMAN'S THERAPY

Gustavo Barcellos

In 1987, a year that celebrated the 25th anniversary of C. G. Jung's death, James Hillman presented—in Milan, at the Italian Center of Analytical Psychology—a reflection on the old master, whereby, together with other equally interesting issues, trying at the same time to absorb, understand, and process it, he argued that the therapy that we inherited from Jung would leave the individual engaged in his daily round "slightly at odds with the daily round, displacing the usual, releasing the captive image and alleviating the suffering of Sophia in the material."[1]

The text of this reflection was published in 1988, in the first issue of the now-extinct British journal of archetypal psychology and art, *Sphinx* (edited by Noel Cobb and Eva Loewe), and is fundamental to comprehend how Hillman understood Jung. In my opinion, this image speaks even more precisely about the therapy that Hillman himself left us as his legacy, which was also called "image focused therapy." Archetypal psychology places us, as patients, and psychology itself as an investigative field, in an essentially critical position, in a slight, albeit constant conflict with all daily things. The expression "slightly" always seemed interesting to me.

Undoubtedly, the first aspect of this "James Hillman therapy"

---

[1] James Hillman, "Jung's Daimonic Inheritance," in *Sphinx: Journal for Archetypal Psychology and the Arts*, volume 1, London: The London Convivium for Archetypal Studies, 1988, p. 18.

is the *therapy of ideas.* As with many others, James Hillman's ideas modified my understanding of psychology, particularly the practice of psychotherapy. Hillman changed our way of thinking and moving ahead with Jungian psychology. It changed our definition of Jungian itself. His thinking goes way beyond psychology, though the latter is both its starting point, and its adversary, paradoxically remaining passionately faithful to it. His work personifies an extraordinary kind of combination of old and new, of tradition and renovation. In other words, Hillman encompasses in himself the *senex* and the *puer* archetypes.

Along the years, the *puer* seems to have been, if not the main theme in his work, certainly the strongest. In it, this archetype appears, not divided (as Hillman himself denounces as happening in culture), but forming a harmonious whole, albeit opened. His work is a beautiful example of pure revolutionary spirit, together with exceptional erudition and solid tradition, revealed by his sources. Through his texts we experience the fresh winds of already established ideas' radical renovation (which can be very disturbing) and, simultaneously, in his numerous notes constantly added to his books, the steady anchor that refers to traditional reflection, that only amplifies arguing and understanding. One that gets involved with the *puer,* gets necessarily involved with the *senex* and, afterward, with *soul.* As few do, Hillman generously opens his sources through those numerous notes, fearless of showing us his walked along paths, so that, should we the reader want to delve further, all roads are open. Hillman proposes an intellectual, albeit not academic, psychology, one that responds to the yearning of the soul for *logos.*

Renovation, the best spirit of *renovatio,* is at the basis of the impulse that generates, among the ideas it presents us, a rebirth of psychology. It is at the basis of the archetypal impulse that wants, let's put it this way, a "re-visioning of psychology." The therapy of ideas is this: to deconstruct and rebuild ideas with which we form our thoughts, thus freeing them to a more imaginative, less conceptual mode. This more imaginative psychology mode starts with Jung and is part of *his* legacy, for, as we know, he personified his concepts, imagined his main psychological ideas as persons. With this, however, Hillman does a therapy for psychology itself, in the sense of deconstructing its concepts, or, quoting Thomas Moore, of remembering that psychology "is not a science or a moral philosophy or a spiritual discipline. It is an imaginative activity of the soul."[2]

Someone already said that James Hillman turns psychology into the investigative arm of poetry. This perception appears in every word of his and is turned into psychological *insight*, carrying the imagination of deep knowledge through a live, active language. The language itself wants to perceive and mirror the creative conscience of the psyche. In addition to being an extraordinary theoretician, Hillman is also an artist with words, intensely preoccupied with the language that expresses his *insights*, intensely conscious, let us put it this way, of the *therapeutic value of the language*, of the talking cure.

Therefore, the importance and value of his thought cannot be totally evaluated without keeping in mind the revolution in the field of psychological ideas that it started, bringing back the Renaissance values we so lack nowadays. Chiefly, in my opinion, this revolution is present in the conception of soul that he brings and defends. Such conception recognizes the soul as a multiple potency, "opening the way to a radical phenomenology of the psyche as an autonomous field of multiple personifications,"[3] to quote now another of Hillman's observations, in that same text, regarding Jung's method and therapy, and, as I see it, perfectly aligned with his own. It is interesting that, in this articulation, this power can be accessed, appreciated, and cultivated by a public that goes way beyond professional psychotherapists. Artists, writers, health professionals, psychoanalysts, teachers, environmental professionals, theologians, philosophers, historians, and social scientists are among those that may amplify considerably the horizons of their reflections and practices. Hillman argues that this potency is fundamentally

---

[2] Thomas Moore in *A Blue Fire: Selected Writings by James Hillman*, introduced and edited by Thomas Moore. New York, NY: HarperPerennial, 1989, p. 16.

[3] James Hillman, "Jung's Daimonic Inheritance." in *Sphinx: Journal for Archetypal Psychology and the Arts*, volume 1, London: The London Convivium for Archetypal Studies, 1988, p. 11.

related to the desire of the knowledge of itself, or self-understanding, that forms the basis of all its manifestations, from art to symptom.

In his written work, themes come and go, as in music. They are not linearly imagined, and, actually, in my opinion, we may read Hillman starting with any of his books, exactly as with Jung's writings. It's a circular route, with many entrances. But, really, it's with the optical metaphor that we have a better understanding of his thought. Hillman's theoretical imagination is, let's say, more visual, rather than tactile or auditory. For the most part, his metaphors are optical: to see, to review, to look, to see through, to consider, to contemplate, to admire. This thought always implies taking another look at his themes, a vision in perspective. (Let's remember that the "look of the Renaissance is called perspective."[4]) Reading him opens the eyes and, thus, also the mind and the heart. I understand that this emphasis in looking is also part of his "therapy," remembering what Alfredo Bosi, the important Brazilian literary critic once said about looking: "Looking is not only directing your eyes to perceive the 'real' outside us. It is often synonym to *caring, guarding, looking after,* actions that bring the Other to the sphere of one's care."[5] Nothing more pertinent to a therapist.

His metaphors are optical, but the rhetoric, I insist, is about disagreement. *Re-Visioning Psychology* is a great book of "No," as if said over and over again: it's *not* that! It's still *not* that! His work was already called a "counter-education," for it separates the mind from its usual convictions. In several senses, it's a subversive psychology, for it subverts what we usually think, our habitual psychological convictions; but, also, for being the "version beneath," the "sub-version," a version of psychology that derives from the bottom point of view, the point of view of the *inferiors*, of the world of darkness, underworld, down there right where the soul is.

My first contact with this "therapy of ideas," in 1985 during the M.A. program at the New School for Social Research in New York, was

---

[4] Alfredo Bosi, "Fenomenologia do Olhar," in *O Olhar*, edited by Adauto Novaes. São Paulo: Companhia das Letras, 2002, p. 74.
[5] Ibid, p. 78.

reading this extraordinary classic presentation of archetypal psychology, the book *Re-Visioning Psychology*. As happened to several people, this reading was a shock, and as well a deep encounter with a psychology of soul. The four verbs that serve as titles to each chapter of this book—"Personifying," "Pathologizing," "Psychologizing," and "Dehumanizing"—while translating and indicating four actions, in fact suggest four more evident ways to soul-making in our lives. The idea is quite simple: once engaged in them, one at a time or all together, a sense of soul, that is, of a significant deepening in ourselves and in the world, expands. We may say that we feel the psychic reality as a live experience. To a good Jungian, that's more than enough.

Another aspect of this "James Hillman therapy," particularly interesting for us in Brazil, is the "South" metaphor and what he made of it, opening new and important theoretical and imaginative ways. Let's consider, to begin with, this text:

> Because the opposition of monotheism and polytheism is so much the baggage of the culture, it is deep in the collective unconscious of each of us. Whatever we say, whatever we write, is so packed with monotheistic assumptions, that an understanding of the polytheistic psyche is almost impossible.[6]

Here, James Hillman dares us to make an effort towards the impossible: understanding the polytheistic psyche, within the monotheistic mind. I do not intend to consider the delicate discussion about the importance of polytheism to psychology. This psychological question, that had, and may still have, much impact in the wish to move psychology, is already amply reflected along the best of his work. The 1981 article "Psychology: Monotheistic or Polytheistic?" from which comes this statement, may be the reference point, the moment he delved more deeply into the matter.

I wrote about and tried to reflect on the "South" metaphor, and on how it responds to the particular perspective we may imagine in

---

[6] James Hillman, "Psychology: Monotheistic or Polytheistic," appendix to David Miller, *The New Polytheism*. Dallas, TX: Spring Publications, 1981, p. 128.

Brazil in relation with the fundamental questions of psychology and the art of psychotherapy. Well, James Hillman helped us see through this metaphor, and think about the "south" as an imaginative attribute of the soul of the world. He gave us "the way to the south" in psychology, and was the first to make us see the richness and the eros of this connection between the south and the soul. We owe him that.

In Brazil, of course, we are inclined to see "south" as still a great metaphor for depth psychology in general. We cannot escape the feeling of "south," into which we are born. So we need to reflect upon it, that is, create ever new images. The mythologem "New," for instance—New World, new land, new continent—as well as the mythologem "Antarctic" (from the Latin *antarcticu*), although we may be still trapped in them, are no longer sufficient, no longer speak to the soul; or, did they ever? "Newness" is the *prison* of the Americas, as James Hillman pointed out so surely;[7] and "Antarctic"—not-Arctic, anti-Arctic, anti-north—is, of course, the rhetoric of negation. Thus the mythologem "South" can be more affirmative, and would have more to say about soul to the theoretical imagination of archetypal psychology.

Archetypal psychology has brought back this metaphor in particular, "south," to make a major theoretical move. This move has to do with the turning of the West-East axis into a North-South axis, which for Jungian psychology meant that we no longer had to go East to go deep. This "south" was meant to be essentially the Mediterranean culture—from Greek myths and religion to Renaissance civilization, philosophy, and modes of living: imaginal sources which brought sensual as well as tragic perspectives to psychology and to psychotherapy. By moving this axis, archetypal psychology contributed to raising our consciousness regarding how we had formulated psychology as "emerg[ing] from the Protestantism of northern and western Europe and its extension westward into North America,"[8] and that we needed to head for the south of the Mediterranean culture, for

---

[7] James Hillman, "Culture and the Animal Soul," *Spring* 62. Woodstock, CT: Spring Publications, 1997.

[8] James Hillman, *Re-Visioning Psychology*, New York, NY: HarperPerennial, 1975, p. 219.

the Classic myths, so as to re-meet soul, beauty, and pathos.

We all know the significance and the power of the south metaphor: it is truly archetypal. Since Freud and the early days of psychoanalysis, it was *the* place to go when imagining a direction towards the unconscious, towards soul: the vertical direction. To find soul we go downwards: personal memories, childhood, ancient myths, complexes, archetypal reality—all this is imagined to be stored deep down inside, the "south" of ourselves. True character is also imagined to be down inside our acts. And we must not forget this "south" stands as well for the lower part of the body.

From a page of his famous 1982 article, "*Anima Mundi*: The Return of the Soul to the World," I want to remember this paragraph:

> Awakening the imagining, sensing heart would move psychology itself from mental reflection toward cordial reflex. Psychology may then become again Florentine; for the move "southward" that I have been urging this last twenty years— from the clinics of Zurich and Vienna, from the white laboratories and black forests of Germany, from the positivist and empiricist dissections of Britain and America, to say nothing of the gymnastics of the tongue in France—cannot be accomplished without moving as well the seat of the soul from brain to heart and the method of psychology from cognitive understanding to aesthetic sensitivity.[9]

We all know those dark projections that landed below the Equator (the Equator, that abstract line of the spirit that does not really *equate* anything): tropical-south as irrational, sexually free, Dionysian, pagan, perverse, archetypally mother-bound due to an extravagant and extraordinary appeal of nature and climate, instinctive, irresponsible, lazy, cannibalistic. What was at first perceived by the *conquistadores* as heavenly, a paradisiacal projection, soon turned into a hellish project to steal, to usurp, and to abuse land and people in the Tropics—gold rush,

---

[9] James Hillman, *The Thought of the Heart and the Soul of the World*, Dallas, TX: Spring Publications, 1993, pp. 108-109.

wood traffic, slavery, soul mutilation.

In Brazil we are well aware of all this, for we too start in the South. My impression is that, beyond Mediterranean culture, this "therapy of James Hillman" can allow this archetypal "south" to be re-imagined. Brazilian South-American syncretic polytheistic culture shines and, in itself, continues to offer a challenge for psychology regarding "south" as a cultural, ethnic, and imaginal location, a region of the soul, beyond what it has already acknowledged as "south." I am trying to suggest that beyond what Hillman showed us of value for psychology in Mediterranean classical culture, cultures below the Equator (such as Brazilian culture) can help archetypal psychology continue to imagine even more radically its fundamental metaphorical direction in thought and research, in an even more radical movement towards the receptive and fecund aspects of soul. This, for us, *functions* therapeutically.

One way to understand it is as a clear result of the melting of the three absolutely different races that originally combined to form Brazilian people: the American Indian, the Portuguese, and the African slave. Alchemy again, *coniunctio* as *solutio*. Miscegenation. And it is clear to me that *miscegenation* is the main contribution to psychology from Brazil. It represents a totally different style of consciousness, more inclusive and receptive, less abstract and conceptual. And it is for psychology a chance to overcome what Hillman refers to as "white supremacy"[10]—ego psychology, empiricism, subjectivism, spiritualism. . . it represents a true "descent into the south."

I'd like to finish with still another aspect of this "Hillman therapy," an aspect which, together with my first observations on a "slightly at odds" consciousness, makes me consider the idea of a "porous ego." This, as a follow-up to the "porous prose" that Augusto de Campos, our most anti-critical concrete poet, dreamed of, de Campos who also was always "in disagreement," following Buckminster Fuller's "ventilated prose." This is a prose intermixed with poetry.

---

[10] James Hillman, "Notes on White Supremacy: Essaying an Archetypal Account of Historical Events." *Spring* 1986. Dallas, TX: Spring Publications.

If ego is to soul what prose is to poetry, maybe we could see in this therapy the image of a "porous ego." The idea of a "ventilated ego" expresses a conscience with a half-opened door. To such a style of consciousness, everything is ventilated, everything offers openings, possibilities, entrances, voids, duplicities. This consciousness is taken along by the *puer*, a consciousness model produced in therapy, a double conscience, "*kairotic*," in two *tempos*, opening fissures in time, thus minimizing its sick and restraining literalism. Back now to this important archetype in his "therapy," I understand that, to Hillman, initiation into the *puer*

> transmits an awareness that individuality is not essentially unity but a doubleness, even a duplicity, and our being is metaphorical, always on two levels at once. Only this twofold truth, *gloria duplex*, can offer protection against shipwreck by teaching us to avoid foundering upon the great monolithic rocks of literal realities. . . . Wherever one is, there is always an "other" by means of whom we reflect existence and because of whom we are always "more", "other", and "beyond" what is here-and-now.[11]

In this sense, considering all of his work, I believe that the books on the *puer are* the key point to get in contact with a "James Hillman therapy." There, individuation is not a cure for division, but rather the *consciousness of division*. Let us remember Jung: "Individuation is becoming that thing which is not the ego, and that is very strange. . . . the self is just the thing which you are not."[12] This makes us face a certain radicalism without which there is no individuation movement, and this radicalism grows with therapy. This radicalism "begins in non-adaptation, that non-conformism or abnormality of idiosyncrasy."[13] In other words, the cure of the division

---

[11] James Hillman, "Pothos," in *Loose Ends: Primary Papers in Archetypal Psychology*. Dallas, TX: Spring Publications, 1975, p. 59.

[12] C. G. Jung, *The Psychology of Kundalini Yoga: Notes of the Seminar Given in 1932*, ed. Sonu Shamdasani, Princeton, NJ: Princeton University Press, 1999, p. 39.

is the consciousness of the division itself, a "sense of duplicity," as he argues, making us not divided individuals, but *doubtful individuals*. These doubtful individuals will always be slightly in disagreement, slightly at odds, slightly in conflict with everything around them.

Quoting Flaubert, imbecility is wanting to conclude. I don't want to conclude anything. We are here to celebrate James Hillman, and I want to do it with the caring abandon we dedicate to someone who taught us so much. For I neither want, nor can I avoid, his shadow—in this context, understanding "shadow" more as his influence, rather than as the Jungian concept. I am here to celebrate him, to pay him tribute as an extraordinary therapist, in his writings, in his work, in his presence. This is why I started playing with those "James Hillman therapies," by way of saying that my phantasy of approaching James Hillman, my James Hillman phantasy, was always that of a *therapist*. Understanding therapy here as the impact he has on us, the throbbing that comes out of each of his pages, the way he moves us.

Gaston Bachelard, the Champagne prophet, the imagination herald, described himself as a psychologist of the books. James Hillman is a psychologist of psychology. Celebrating him is, for the most part, celebrating psychology, the vitality of psychology.

---

[13] James Hillman, "Jung's Daimonic Inheritance," in *Sphinx: Journal for Archetypal Psychology and the Arts*, volume 1, London: The London Convivium for Archetypal Studies, 1988, p. 13.

JAMES HILLMAN:
PHILOSOPHICAL INTIMATIONS

Edward Casey

"Follow curiosity, inquire into important
ideas, risk transgression. This takes
courage, by which I mean letting go of
old ideas and letting go to odd ideas..."

-James Hillman, in conversation: Athens,
2008; while discussing *Aphrodite's Justice*

"Opposition brings concord. Out of discord comes the fairest harmony."[1] James Hillman loved Heraclitus and found him irresistible. I can think of no better way to remember and honor Jim's matchlessly creative work than by allusion to the deeply emblematic Heraclitean theme of the fate of opposition—the vicissitudes of polar differences that, instead of destroying each other, end by giving rise to an unanticipated concord, albeit one that has been concealed throughout the self-sundering itself. If we think only of the characteristic Hillmanian divisions between clinic and world, ego and psyche, imagination and reality, and war and peace, we get a sense of the oppositionalism from which Hillman's always took its rise. An emblematic utterance in this spirit is this one: "In the realm of soul the ego is a paltry thing," we read in the Preface to *Re-Visioning Psychology*[2]—

---

[1] *Heraclitus*, tr. P. Wheelwright (Princeton: Princeton University Press, 1959), Fr. 98.

words that could have been spoken by Heraclitus and that effectively encapsulate the basic message of this major manifesto.

In this talk I will sketch out the theme of pitched tension in Hillman's early work in order to show its transformation into a different key in his writings after 1980, when he began to pursue various forms of tacit convergence and fusion. I will maintain that this became the most fruitful phase of his later work, though one that could not have happened without the first, mainly Martial period.

I

Hillman's thought flourished in the presence of opposites and derived energy from the clash of contradictory directions. For a long time—indeed to the very end—he railed at false compromises and easy solutions. These included some basic parts of Jung's thought: above all, his emphasis on achieving balance, wholeness, and especially "monotheism" in one of Hillman's most enduring battle cries. Who can forget the fulminations in *Re-Visioning Psychology*, his first all-out and still most defiant statement of principle in the founding of archetypal psychology from the ashes of Jungian pieties? This brave and bold breakthrough book has for its targets not so much his predecessors in depth psychology as the obsession with simplicity or system—in particular, with the three primary patterns of centrism, syncretism, and unificationism.

Notice the rhetoric of *Re-Visioning Psychology* itself: resolutely nay-saying, neither this nor that, *neti neti* as the medievals liked to say. One sample from among many: "As archetypal psychology is not a science or a religion, so too it is not a humanism."[3] NOT. . . NOT. . . NOT. Recall Hillman's insistence throughout this passionately angry book that soul-making is NOT a matter of strengthening the ego: the goal of the "ego psychology" that flourished in the wake of Freud (and that was equally the target of Jacques Lacan). We must "work out a

---

[2] Hillman, *Re-Visioning Psychology* (New York: HarperPerennial, 1975), p. xvi.
[3] *RP*, p. 171.

psychology that is not centered in the ego, not centered anywhere."[4] The literal ego-centrism of much of ego psychology as well as the Self-centrism of Jung's thought were equally refused by the Hillman of this period in favor of an ec-centric vector, a fleeing from the temptation to make *centration* itself the goal of psychological process.

An equal but opposite error is the *syncretism* that tempts system-builders in every field, very much including philosophy in its metaphysical moments. Getting it all together, whether in one's life or one's thought, is NOT the goal. Depth psychology teaches us that life is continually falling apart: this is the lesson of the "pathologizing" that is such a prominent theme in *Re-Visioning*. The symptomatology that was the starting point for Freud and Jung alike did not signify sickness but the fragmentation of the self to which all human beings are liable: "the necessity of pathologizing."[5] Hillman underlines what Jung and Freud first insisted on: "the symptom," wrote Freud in his *Introductory Lectures*, is "a thing that is more foreign to the ego than anything else in the mind." He adds to this basic cleavage, this inherent anti-syncretism the idea, tacit in his predecessors' theories, that pathologizing is not to be cured or "treated" but made to *yield meaning*: "only when things fall apart do they open up into new meanings. . . a new significance dawn[s]."[6] The double negation of the not. . . not gives rise to an affirmation of what something *means*—means in the light of the archetypes that are the nodal points of the complexes identified by Jung as lying at the core of symptomatic behavior.

The very multiplicity of archetypes points to a third direction resisted vehemently by the Hillman of the Terry Lectures. He was concerned to oppose all monothetic theories, philosophical or psychological: all theories that posited the One or Unity as an absolute or controlling term, as in the systems of Parmenides, certain strands in Plato, and much of Plotinus. Over against the deep temptation to find a definitive term that unifies all disparities, Hillman proposed diversity itself as the deeper truth. Versus the One, undercutting it, is *the Many*.

---

[4] Ibid, p. 187.
[5] Ibid, p. 104.
[6] Ibid, p. 111.

Plato himself had struggled to get there in his "esoteric" teachings, for instance, in his idea of the "indefinite dyad." But this latter notion, promising as it is, is posited in view of an overarching unification: for the dyad contains the One *and* the Many, the Like and the Unlike, the Odd and the Even, the Same and the Different. Hillman unblinkingly endorses the Many, the Odd, the Different, and the Unlike—in a deliberate effort to upend the Western metaphysical passion for unification at all costs: as the *unio mentalis*, the one God, the ego as *número uno*, the one right way to live, the one best way to achieve mental health, etc. The One has to go; the Many must be embraced: the "much at once," as William James put it: much too much for reductive systems of thought.

II

We can regard *Re-Visioning* as clearing the ground of major simplifications that obscure what is in fact a very complicated scene. The patterns just mentioned must be undercut before moving on. But undercut by what? Moving on to what? Derrida said that once false binaries are deconstructed, we can affirm "dissemination."[7] Is that, or its equivalent, what Hillman is asking us to do—to move from sheer outright opposition to disarray? Or is there a more constructive alternative?

Any adequate answer to these questions must take into account something very special about James Hillman as a depth psychologist: *He brought philosophy to bear on psychology in major and unique ways.* This is one of his most distinctive gifts to the field. Freud eschewed philosophy after his student days—when he won a school debate on the question of whether Materialism is true (not surprisingly, he argued that it *is*)—and even if he wrote and thought from philosophical presumptions (such as the nature of consciousness or the character of reality that informs the "reality principle"), he was unwilling to own up

---

[7] See Jacques Derrida, *Positions* (1982), interview with Julia Kristeva.

to them. Jung was more explicit in his philosophical allegiances, as we can see in the Glossary to *Psychological Types*, where Plato, Aristotle, and Kant figure prominently; this is not to mention his ongoing intensive seminar on Nietzsche's *Thus Spake Zarathustra*. But he balked at endorsing any given philosophical system, and he certainly did not think of himself as a philosophical psychologist.

James Hillman may not have applied this latter epithet to himself either, but the presence of philosophy in his work is pervasive throughout its evolution. His undergraduate concentration at Trinity College, Dublin, was in philosophy, with a special focus on the British empiricists, particularly Berkeley and Hume. His doctorate from the University of Zurich—published as *Emotion*, his first book—was expressly Aristotelian in its employment of the four basic causes (efficient, final, formal, and material) as structuring principles for a new understanding of affects and feelings. Nietzsche is prominent in the deep probing of the contrast between the Apollonian and the Dionysian that is so salient in *The Myth of Analysis* and *Re-Visioning Psychology*. And the move to *anima mundi* in the early 1980's took flight on the wings of the idea of the "World Soul" in Plato's *Timaeus* and Plotinus's *Enneads: anima mundi* is unthinkable without these ancient philosophical precedents. Indeed, the return to the Renaissance for inspiration that is such a forceful feature of *Re-Visioning* meant a renewed appreciation of "the School of Athens" on the part of figures like Pico della Mirandola and Giordano Bruno—and of James Hillman in Zurich. Neo-Platonism was the not so hidden motor of philosophy and art alike in the Italian Renaissance, and it is not surprising that an epigraph from Plotinus is placed at the opening of the chapter on "Psychologizing or Seeing Through" in *Re-Visioning Psychology*: "Our general instinct to seek and learn will, in all reason, set us inquiring into the nature of the instrument with which we search."[8]

For those who knew James personally, it was always a marvel to behold his wide-ranging mind swing freely between philosophical ideas and depth-psychological sources with ease and even nonchalance—as if

---

[8] (cited at *RP*, p. 113 from the *Enneads* IV, 3, 1).

it were self-evident that understanding, say, psychological necessity requires an invocation of *Ananke,* the goddess of Necessity, as she is invoked in Plato's *Timaeus.*[9]

James and I became fast friends from the day of our first meeting on the occasion of the Terry Lectures in 1972—when I did not hesitate to heap philosophical questions on him. We continued intense discussions during the next year in New Haven when I helped to arrange a visiting lectureship for him in the Psychology Department: little did his colleagues in that department realize what a subversive force they had among them! During that time, the fall of 1973, we debated issues that were central to the composition of the final text of *Re-Visioning Psychology.* We talked heatedly in the kitchen of a small apartment which he and Pat Berry had rented on Chapel St. in New Haven. Fully twenty years later, we were still talking on Chapel St.: I recall a long conversation on issues of character (*The Force of Character and the Lasting Life,* published in 1999, was in its germinal stage) on which he took extensive notes. When we reached my car, he realized that he no longer had these notes: we returned to the restaurant where we had talked for three hours: they were nowhere to be found; next we scoured the street, including the trash baskets on its sidewalks, acting like bums from a Beckett play; all to no avail. Admitting defeat, we tried to reconstruct the main points of the conversation as we drove east toward Thompson, well aware that a full reconstruction was not possible.

We shared a deep admiration for the poetry of Wallace Stevens, who was for both of us the quintessential philosophical poet—to be set alongside Lucretius and Dante and Goethe, the philosophical poets discussed by George Santayana in *Three Philosophical Poets*: a book that had moved us both when we were younger.

---

[9] See the essay, "From Athene, Ananke, and the Necessity of Abnormal Psychology" (presented at the Eranos Conference, August 1974, and first published as "On the Necessity of Abnormal Psychology" in *Eranos Yearbook* 43 (1974). Reprinted, with corrections, in *Facing the gods,* ed. J. Hillman (Dallas: Spring Publications, 1980). Now in Hillman, James. *Mythic figures.* Uniform Edition, v. 6.1, Putnam: Spring, 2007. Freud, it will be recalled, alludes to Ananke in his *Beyond the Pleasure Principle* (1920).

Just as poetry and philosophy join forces in these epic poets (as also in T. S. Eliot, another poet we both esteemed), so I like to think that James Hillman brought philosophy and psychology together in equally epic ways. Hence my delight when James asked me to write the Preface to Volume Eight of his *Uniform Edition*. To be titled *Philosophical Intimations*, this will contain those writings—essays and fragments—that explicitly conjoin philosophical and psychological thinking. Even in his last weeks of life, we discussed with Margot MacLean what might go into this volume. Earlier, James had preferred the title *Philosophical Inclinations*, but as we talked, "intimations" seemed to capture better the sense of the volume, which not only captures the author's life-long draw to philosophy but his slowly dawning sense that philosophy offers intimations that are of particular value for archetypal psychology.

III

In working on this volume—which will feature mostly later, unpublished essays—I have been struck by several titles that yoke together things that are usually considered incompatible with each other. Incompatible in the eyes of classical depth psychology or classical philosophy, and often by both. Without straining after paradox for its own sake, these essays *show* what their titles *say*. At the level of literal saying, their title themes are manifestly oxymoronic. But in the careful exploration of these themes they exhibit, and finally justify, what their incongruous titles brazenly announce. In this way, they move beyond the overt oppositionalism—the martial stance, the puer position—of most of the author's earlier work: toward a direction that is at once philosophical and psychological—to the point that this late phase of Hillman's thinking itself moves to the unlikely marriage of these two fields, so often held apart from each other. In this way, the very early Hillman (the erstwhile student of philosophy) is re-incarnated in the final stage of an extraordinary career as an iconoclastic psychologist. If I am right, the last iconoclasm consists in deconstructing the myth of philosophy and psychology as separate disciplines.

I shall begin with an account of "Aphrodite's Justice," the essay from which the small book of this same title stemmed. What could Aphrodite, the goddess of Beauty, have to do with Justice, the domain of Hera and Diké? The oxymoronic combination of Aphrodite with Justice juxtaposes two matters that are usually considered incompatible with each other. Doesn't beauty engage us in the domain of pleasure and taste, surely very subjective matters? And does not justice concern what holds objectively for all who fall under its jurisdiction; if this were not the case—if it obtains for some rather than for others—it's a sham: it is *injustice*. Justice must be distributed equally, whereas beauty is differentially located: some things, whether people or artworks or landscapes, are endowed with it, others lack it. Not everyone is equally beautiful, but justice in the form of fair laws applies to all who fall subject to it.

If this is so, how can Hillman speak of *Aphrodite's Justice*? Whose justice? Whose beauty? How can these contraries combine? The essay, first delivered as a talk in Capri in 2007, was published in 2008 by a Naples publishing house as a small pink book with facing English and Italian pages. [10] This was to be Hillman's last book, and the theme could not have been more appropriate as an *envoi*—given his early concern with beauty and love in *The Myth of Analysis* and his increasing draw to questions of political and environmental justice in the last decade of his life. It was as if he were taking leave of his readers by a re-visitation and radical re-doing of what he had already done in such intriguing ways

---

[10] "Beyond Beauty and Justice," a third late topic was announced in a special address at Rimini in 2001 under the auspices of the President of the Italian Republic: Destiny. This was never to be fully explored, though a late talk on Oedipus he gave in Manhattan at my invitation in 2005 bore on issues of fate and destiny in *Oedipus Rex*. All we hear of this unfinished project in the small pink book is that "these three classical principles [of Beauty, Justice, and Destiny] with mythic proportions are deeper and more appropriate to the soul's concern than any other trivium of concepts such as Nature, Nurture, and Individuality, or Reason, Will, and Emotion, or Ego, Id, and Superego; or even those ancient three *nous, psyche,* and *physis,* which we today name as Mind, Soul, and Body." (*La Giustizia di Afrodite/Aphrodite's Justice* [Edizioni La Conchiglia, Capri, 2008], p. 14).

fully thirty years earlier.[11]

Aphrodite's Justice undertakes to show how justice and beauty belong together despite the received view that they inhabit altogether different domains: beauty being concerned with form, charm, and seduction; justice with order, measure, retribution. Hillman's argument proceeds by first pointing to all the ostensible differences between these dichotomous topics and then undermining the dichotomy by showing the fierce bonding and finally the identity between Beauty and Justice.

The separation between these two great themes is profound and is attributed to the combined effects of Christianity and the Platonic and post-Platonic tradition in philosophy. We recognize Hillman's impassioned denunciation of any such separation in this vivid passage:

> Venus has been trapped in a basic Christian dilemma that divides beauty from goodness and truth, splitting the classical idea of *kalokagathon*—beauty and goodness held in one term. After splitting them from each other, importance is given to the moral order, which sets up Venus as an immoral disturbance, an outlaw. She becomes Carmen, a destructive temptress. The long history of Christianized philosophy has driven ethics from aesthetics, Justice from Beauty, so that we customarily believe that you cannot be both good and beautiful, ethical and alluring; nor can the pleasures of the senses be the path to truth.[12]

---

[11] Ibid., p. 14. Note that Elaine Scarry published a book titled *On Beauty and Being Just* in 1999. Not referred to in Hillman's text, this small text takes up comparable yet very different ways in which the presence of beauty brings with it an acute sense of justice. (See Elaine Scarry, *On Beauty and Being Just* [Princeton: Princeton University Press, 1999], esp. pp. 12-33.) Especially striking is the convergence between the two authors in their insistence that beauty is to be found in the particular, not in the general: "Beauty always takes place in the particular" (*On Beauty and Being Just*, p. 18); beauty is found in the "*exact particulars of sensuous display*" (*Aphrodite's Justice*, p. 48; his italics). Heraclitus already said, "Men who love wisdom should acquaint themselves with a great many particulars" (Fr. 3; Wheelwright).

[12] Ibid., p. 26.

Philosophy, especially when it becomes the ally of institutionalized religion, presents us with the spectacle wherein reason triumphs over love—and beauty is banished from both. Love and beauty are delivered over to literalism, which already in *Re-Visioning Psychology* is Hillman's Enemy #1.[13] And his philosophical enemy is Descartes, with his "insistence on clear and distinct ideas [that underlie a] compartmentalized literalistic psychology."[14] For Descartes as earlier for the Church fathers, when it comes to Beauty and Justice never will their twain meet.

How to *see through* this literal dilemma? Hillman offers two paths. The first is the more direct. He states, unequivocally, the inextricable imbrication of justice and beauty, speaking of "the full impact of beauty [in] its power (*peitho*) to move the heart toward both love and justice."[15] It is this power that is betrayed when justice is set apart from beauty.

The other path is through myth: to move past this dilemma, we must "turn back to mythic figures in search of Aphroditic Justice."[16] This small pink book presents a potpourri of such figures, who bear on the internal relationship between Beauty and Justice: among them, Nemesis, the Horae, the Graces, the Fates. These "complicate" the figure of Aphrodite, thus "make our appreciation of her more subtle, and yet intensify her effects by fusing the multiple strands into a more compacted tension."[17] Aphrodite herself embodies such things as "fittingness, the rightful place, a delightful justness, the pleasure of order."[18] Here we get to the heart of the matter: *if beauty is conceived*

---

[13] "The control of rationalism over the investigations gives little mind to love. . . Love becomes a love without beauty, a moral imperative, a 'should' not an urge. . . These rationalistic separations into specific topics—each with Big Letters—Love. Desire. Beauty. Justice—are studied separately in academia and treated separately in philosophic encyclopedias, holding our Western minds that have abandoned their mythic roots, fast in the walled compartments of literalism" (Ibid., pp. 38-40).

[14] Ibid., p. 40

[15] Ibid.

[16] Ibid., p. 28.

[17] Ibid., p. 58.

[18] Ibid., p. 48.

as the fitting and the suitable, its alliance with justice becomes much more accessible. This is what is expressed in the common English phrase "poetic justice," which signifies that there is a certain felicity (as well as irony) in the working of justice. In this same spirit, the very concept of *kosmos* in the original sense of this word alludes to the marriage of beauty and order: as Hillman avers, *kosmos* "connotes both aesthetic and ethical order, both adornment and decency."[19] If the cosmos is aphroditic—if it is beautiful in its appearances—this is only because it is composed of judicious orderings, ways of being just. In this vision, "the walls between the ethical and the aesthetic dissolve."[20]

Nevertheless, distinctions are woven into this aesthetic/ethical nexus—distinctions, for instance, between Venus and Aphrodite, Love and Beauty, Diké and Themis—but never with the intention of holding the distinguished terms apart permanently. The passion is for precision, not for prescinding: distinctions are not separations. The existence of distinguishable strands within Beauty and Justice alike serve only to bind them together all the more fiercely into "a more compacted tension." In the end, if "all behaviors and characters are fitting [and] find their place in the cosmos,"[21] they do so because their just positioning is aphroditic: attractive, comely, "aesthetic." They all belong to Beauty—or rather, they bring forth beauty itself in the multiplicity of its manifold guises, in "its full confusing reach."[22]

James Hillman has here accomplished what we can call a *delicate undoing* of divisive dualisms that have kept the mind of modernity in its characteristically schizoid state, sundered from itself. Both Beauty and Justice—and the one because the other—act to subvert this disempowered, schismatic paralysis. In this way, he dives under the dichotomizing rhetoric of the Jeremiads that render his earlier writings so seductive. We can now see that this rhetoric is mimetic with the very separatisms he was committed to seeing through: he was fighting fire

---

[19] Ibid., p. 50.

[20] Ibid., p. 52. Hillman adds "attention to aesthetics is ethical behavior and ethical behavior is an aesthetic display" (ibid.).

[21] Ibid., p. 74.

[22] Ibid., p. 58.

with fire. But once the fires have abated and the battles have been won, he can shift through the ashes and attain a level of insight that was not available in the assumption of more bellicose stances.

IV

Another late essay has the antinomic title "On Psychological Knowledge."[23] It challenges us to ask ourselves: how can *knowledge* be *psychological*? Does not established and verified *knowledge* stand above or beyond the merely psychological? In his *Logical Investigations,* Husserl went to considerable lengths to argue that the laws of logic are untouched by what he called "psychologism," the belief that the truth of an inference or the content of a proposition is a function of how we happen to think about it—that it is a creature of psychological acts of thinking or believing. Not so! exclaimed Husserl. Knowing the truth cannot be reduced to thinking the truth. Knowledge as certain and systematic cannot be reduced to any mere activity of the cognizing psyche.

Hillman revises this seemingly plausible claim of Husserl's by showing in detail how the psyche is always already engaged in knowing—but knowing of another kind from that at stake in ordinary cognition. Just as knowledge is not only logical or scientific, so psyche not only cognizes (and recognizes) the surrounding world but is, still more, a power of feeling and connecting. In this way, he seeks to bear out in our time the truth of another Heraclitean fragment: "You could not discover the limits of soul, even if you traveled every road to do so; such is the depth of its meaning."[24]

"On Psychological Knowledge" was delivered in Modena, Italy, in September 2007, the same year (indeed the same month) as *Aphrodite's Justice* was presented in Capri. This essay undertakes a deconstruction

---

[23] "On Psychological Knowledge," unpublished essay. The reference numbers below refer to manuscript pages. The essay will eventually be published in vol. 8 of the *Uniform Edition* which I am editing and writing a preface for.

[24] *Heraclitus,* Fr. 42.

of knowledge as "knowledge *about*" the psyche—that is, approximate knowing from an external point of view, as in experimental psychology or the artificial categories of the *DSM*—so as to undertake an analysis in depth of what Hillman calls "knowledge *of* the soul" and of "knowledge *in* the soul." Knowledge of the soul covers what we can be said to know from within such as certain moral virtues, including justice; ultimately, the scope of such internal knowledge exceeds anything we can express in words, much less tabulate in numbers. If the first kind of knowing, knowing about, is external to soul, the second kind stems from the unfathomable depths of soul; it is a knowing/unknowing of matters that pertain to soul which exceed the ability of soul itself to delineate or understand them. If the first model gives us too much—too much unsorted knowledge: a mess of pottage, as it were—the second gives us too little: it gives us psychic truths but leaves us in ignorance and epistemological uncertainty.

The stage is now set for knowledge *in* the soul: knowledge uniquely exercised by soul, *its own knowledge*, "psychic knowledge in itself."[25] To the unknowing that is the outcome of the second kind of knowledge, we add a form of knowing that has its own distinctive shape. One of its characteristic shapes is "recollection": *anamnesis* in Plato's term for calling upon universals that are innate to soul and not learned from individual experience (these are the predecessors of "archetypes" in Jung's sense of the term). These universals are not vapid concepts but concretely structured individual things. Hillman agrees with Plotinus's elaboration of such knowledge of universals as giving the basis for "the inherent intelligibility of all things."[26] But Hillman finds the roots of such intelligibility to reside in the underworld of shades and shadows—the realm that Plato had disparaged as mere *eikasia*, the debased region of icons, mere images. For Hillman, on the contrary, it is precisely by means of images that we come to know the archetypal source of all things:

It is the image that instigates the psyche's knowledge drive, that

---

[25] "On Psychological Knowledge," p. 7
[26] Ibid., p. 10

desire to go beyond self-satisfaction with its own images. They are not its knowledge, only its propaedeuticum. Evidently images need an intimacy with something beyond themselves, a close companionship with the intellectual principle. Then, an image is enhanced with archetypal significance and knows itself as belonging to, at home, in the intelligence of the cosmos.[27]

This intriguing statement sketches out a dimension of Hillman's later thought that we witness emerging in the last years of his life—a linking of archetypal psychology not only with image but with a principle of intelligibility that is vast in scope. Psyche is no longer self-enclosed, but is returned to the world wherein it finds its own unique way of knowing embedded and exemplified, as when we read that "the image is the archetype's own pregnancy, [the archetype] contained within the image as its intelligibility."[28] It follows that "our souls are made of intelligence; they are knowledge."[29]

We need to pause and ponder the major step that is here taken. Images alone no longer suffice, as in Jung's axiomatic utterance that Hillman cited so often in his early work: "image is psyche." Nor is it enough to speak of "image-sense," as in the title of that remarkable group of essays he published in *Spring* in the late 1970's. The sense of images is not endemic or unique to them alone; this sense draws upon principles of intelligibility rooted *in* the soul—in its own internal knowledge. If phenomenology (on which Hillman always kept a wary eye) would insist on the bodily and earthly origin of images—the dimension *from under*—Hillman now insists on the intelligible source of images *from above*. He edges toward metaphysics by taking a step beyond cosmology, toward what is "beyond-the-physical" as the word "meta-physical" literally signifies.

In our last prolonged conversations, he wanted to pursue just one question: "*Where* do images come from?" This is a question about ultimate sources, not about direct experience or psychological import.

---

[27] Ibid.

[28] Ibid., p. 11.

[29] Ibid.

At one point in our conversations in the spring of 2009, he remarked with a startle: "Ed, we must be talking metaphysics!" He was at once surprised and pleased to realize this. He was returning to philosophy after having been on so many amazing journeys in depth psychology. But he continued to seek soul—now in the form of intelligible knowledge held within the soul and at the root of psychically significant images.

If this turning to the metaphysical sounds ponderous or escapist to you, have no worry. Hillman was not interested in devising a new *system* of metaphysics with an elaborate architectonic structure. He remained mercurial in the very midst of the metaphysical. We see this in his insistence that knowledge in the soul proceeds by instantaneous "insightings," which are as "fluid as the soul itself, ephemeral acts of immediate precision."[30] Plato, the first metaphysical thinker in the West after Parmenides, here joins forces with Hillman: metaphysical insight comes "suddenly, like a blaze of light (*phos*) kindled by a leaping spark. . . generated in the soul and. . . self-sustaining."[31] For Hillman, however, such blazing insight arrives in the guise of an image, not a Form, an *eidos*. "I have searched into myself," says Heraclitus in still another fragment[32] and what this search yields are phosphorescent images that escort us into the archetypal, cosmic, and metaphysical dimensions of everything that is.

Hillman also remains *grounded* in this late searching after metaphysical knowledge. It may come from on high, but intelligibility does not mean anything high-falutin or fancy. Thus Hillman rejects the "transcendental" path of locating archetypal universals in an ethereal other-world, "a remote supernal realm."[33] He insists that images and their metaphysical resonances are both located in *this* world, down here below where their sightings occur. He might have quoted Rilke at this

---

[30] Ibid.

[31] Plato, the Seventh Letter, section 341c.

[32] Freeman, *Ancilla to Pre-Socratic Philosophers: A Complete Translation of the Fragments in Diels, Fragmente de Vorsokratiker* (Cambridge: Harvard University Press, 1983), Fr. 8.

[33] "On Psychological Knowledge," p. 12.

point: "Hiersein ist herrlich" ("being-*here* is the wonder").[34]

Near the end of "On Psychological Knowledge," he invokes a lioness who lies in wait to spring on a gazelle: her knowledge is wholly kinaesthetic and links her body to a field in which the gazelle appears as a desirable prey. The *notitia* of the lion is a "carnal knowledge" that is "the close companion of the image and [the] archetype, an intimacy in the flesh with the prey."[35] We witness here an animal "psyche in action. . . [with] a 'direct perception' of the field's intelligibility. . . She *is* her knowledge, a knowledge in soul of a knowledgeable being: a *gnosis*."[36] We have here the assertion not just of the general thesis of *anima mundi*, the great expansive step of Hillman's thought in the 1980's, but now more specifically the positing of a *knowing animal soul* that animates the field of perception and dexterous action, thus a soul that is no longer merely or mainly human.

In this remarkable late text on psychological knowledge—ranging from the human to the animal and back again in the context of embodied knowledge—Hillman says suddenly that "we are [now] being tempted toward metaphysical epistemology."[37] He is so tempted because it is only by recourse to a metaphysical realm of embodied universals that the epistemology of the psyche, its knowing of the world and itself, proceeds by bounding leaps of insight. "The lion springs only once": this is a saying that Freud cited with relish. So too James Hillman, at the end, springs into metaphysics from the *archai* of psychological knowledge in depth.

V

In his Forward to a recent translation of Heraclitean fragments, Hillman speaks of the "poetics of dissonance" he finds in these fulgurating fragments.[38] Perhaps we could speak similarly of a

[34] Seventh *Duino Elegy*, tr. A. S. Kline, 2001.
[35] "On Psychological Knowledge," p. 13.
[36] Ibid.
[37] Ibid, p. 12.
[38] *Fragments: The Collected Wisdom of Heraclitus*, tr. B. Haxton (New York:

"philosophy of dissonance" that manifests itself in apparently incompatible pairs of concepts such as Beauty and Justice, Psyche and Knowledge. In this light, Hillman can be seen as propounding in his later work the post-modern equivalents of Heraclitean conundra. Hillman takes us back to Heraclitus by standing on the shoulders of Plato and Plotinus—and Proclus, who first proposed the technique of *epistrophê*, the reversion of the soul to its archetypal base. He looks back from these Promethean predecessors, and only by so doing does he look forward to his own Epimethean vision. It is by this return to the Milesian and Athenian roots of Western thought (and to his own beginnings in studying philosophy at Trinity College, Dublin) that he attains such leaping insight into the nascent structures of an increasingly global culture in his later writings on the environmental and the political. He gains purchase on the psychological and planetary future by touching base with a philosophical past that has a narrow geographical and cultural base.

Just as Heraclitus finds consonance in depth underlying dissonance on the surface, so Hillman discovers a comparable deep consonance underneath manifest dissonance. For both figures—one situated at the birth of philosophical thinking in the West, the other in the far end of psychological reflection—"the hidden harmony is better than the obvious."[39] But the hidden does not just lie concealed under a surface; it is something *wrought* out of what is un-hidden—from the very oppositions set out expressly at surfaces wrought with words and concepts.

We return here to where we began, with this gnomic utterance: "Opposition brings concord. Out of discord comes the fairest harmony." Suggested here is a much more radical model than that of two layers merely juxtaposed, as with the manifest and the latent in Freud's model of dreams. Hillman's model of the psyche is importantly different from the view that the manifest is generated from the latent. Quite the converse: the deeper level, that of the hidden harmony, comes forth from the manifest itself.

Penguin Classics, 2003), p. xvi.

[39] *Fragments*, tr. Haxton, Fr. 116.

"The depths are on the surface," said Wittgenstein in a statement of which Hillman was especially fond. But equally the deep arises *from* the surface—from the world of first impressions, bare appearances, and casual glances. ("The world is revealed only in quick glances," says Hillman in the same Forward to Heraclitus.[40]) Here we descend into the deeper logic of knowledge and beauty alike—the informal logic that precedes the formal logic of manipulated signs.

Thereby as well we enter into a realm where philosophy and psychology belong together in a tangled skein of conjoint activity, in a dense realm where they are partners in one and the same generative enterprise. What is this enterprise? It is *depth psychology conceived as a philosophy of the depths derived from surfaces.* Philosophy and psychology, so closely akin in Hillman's life and thought, converge in his late writings in the form of a suggested new discipline: a *psycho-philosophy* that is as promising as it is perplexing.

Conclusion

Rather than seeing incompatibility between the various paired terms at stake in the three dyads I have discussed as they come forward in Hillman's last writings (Beauty and Justice, Knowledge and Psyche, and I add: Philosophy and Psychology), let us say that the members of each pair call for one another, indeed *require* each other—desperately. Each member is *sine qua non* for the other. Rather than forcing us to choose between them, both terms are needed for each to become what its own deeper meaning entails—a meaning that arises from the very surface of their ostensible differences. Only from discord can we come to the unsuspected concord that James Hillman reached at the end of his time on earth.

---

[40] Foreward to *Fragments*, p. xvi.

ARCHETYPAL ASTROLOGY:
AN INTRODUCTION

Laurence Hillman[1]

"We know that the wildest and most moving dramas are played not in the theatre but in the hearts of ordinary men and women."
C. G. Jung[2]

Since ancient times we have looked to the heavens for guidance: from navigating the seas, to aligning calendars with solar and lunar cycles, to following the bright star of Bethlehem towards Nazareth—even to the millions of people who read their horoscopes in magazines every day. Nowadays most of us completely lack any sense of wonderment and magic when we relate to the natural world, but stepping outside into the night can change all of that. The skies have been filled with stories for as long as human beings have been watching

---

[1] **Editors' Note:** Laurence and his father gave a presentation titled "Venus in America" in San Francisco in 1997. According to Laurence, "My father and I travel through psychology, philosophy, history, astrology, and the arts. Discussions with workshop participants on Venusian issues, both archetypal and personal. Themes include: What happened to Venus when she arrived on US shores? How did Venus manifest in original native cultures? Why is therapy so obsessed with relationships? Why is our divorce rate so high and our support for the arts so low? We address architecture, beauty, food, flowers, design, clothing, love, romance, and pornography, to only name a few. Just about anyone will find some extraordinary tidbit in this only existing recording of my father and I working together." The recording can be purchased at Laurence's website, http://www.lhillman.com/.

[2] "New Paths in Psychology" (1912) in *Collected Works 7, Two Essays in Analytical Psychology*, p. 425.

the heavens—and perhaps longer. Every major culture has included celestial stories in its mythology, and several have created a complex astrology where the movement of the planets against the background of the celestial firmament was recorded and given meaning. Gazing into a night sky remains awe-inspiring, particularly in times when we see the world increasingly shrinking to monitors that fit into the palm of our hand.

When I look at the sky I see a drama unfolding. I imagine a huge theatre where the planets are the actors on a magnificent stage playing out a grand story. This story has a certain quality to it. I look up and I wonder if we are in a tragedy or in a comedy. What is the next act? Are the curtains about to come down on what is currently playing out? There is a distinct feeling to any moment we live in, a *quality of time*. The ancient Greeks knew this concept as *kairos*. The astrologer reads this quality by the kind of celestial drama playing out in that moment. Each of us still demonstrates our capacity to describe *kairos* when we use expressions such as "there is tension in the air" or "everything is slow today." In its simplest form we can define astrology as *a tool with which to read the quality of time,* in the same way that we would describe the quality of a play.

To make this vast drama more manageable we imagine the planets dropping onto a circular stage on earth, a reflection of the celestial stage. It is circular because in the sky the planets basically move on circular paths. The planets have become actors and are walking around the perimeter of our stage in real time. The Moon, *Queen of the Hearth*, completes her walk in about 28 days. We are familiar with this cycle from one full Moon to another. The Sun, *Lord of Ego*, takes a year to complete his walk, while Pluto, *Lord of the Underworld*, takes about 248 years, and so on. We note a big difference in the speed at which they walk and that they are, of course, moving all the time just like the planets never cease to wander across the heavens. Our circular stage, as a model of the heavens, is a reflection of what is happening in real time in the sky.

At the moment of your birth a particular celestial play was unfolding above your place of birth. Taking this to the personal level, we imagine the earthly stage to be *within* you. We are then "peopled" by these actors. This notion is not strange at all. We often find ourselves saying something akin to, "a part of me wants to do this, but another part of me wants to do that." Our understanding of such an experience would be that two such inner actors are arguing about something and essentially pulling at you from different directions. Jung talks about inner archetypes and in pop-psychology today it is common to use expressions such as the "inner child." These are all similar concepts. With our stage we get an image of these inner figures so commonly referred to in a psychologized world.

At your birth we ask the actors to stand still for a moment and snap a photograph of the stage from above. We then plot this image onto a piece of paper, effectively creating a picture of the heavens at the precise moment of your birth. This picture is referred to as your birth horoscope (*horo-scopos* = hour watching or picture of the hour). We now have an illustration of a dramatic event that we can study; a play with ten characters on a circular stage. To be able to understand and eventually interpret the play we go though four layers in a horoscope. First we need to know the actors. They represent the first layer. There are ten of them and here is a brief introduction:

> **The Sun** – Lord of Ego
> **The Moon** – Queen of the Hearth
> **Mercury** – Lord of Mind
> **Venus** – Goddess of Beauty and Love
> **Mars** – Warrior Lord
> **Jupiter** – Lord of Expansion
> **Saturn** – Master of Discipline
> **Uranus** – Your Inner Disturber
> **Neptune** – Lord of Dreams
> **Pluto** – Lord of the Underworld

Archetypal astrology (there are other fields of astrology) postulates two things.

- Firstly, that *the planets are archetypal in nature and represent universal experiences that we all share.*

- Secondly, *the celestial drama that constellated above you as you drew your first breath continues to play out on your inner stage throughout your life.*

The first postulate is more easily understood. It is based on the worldview that nature is not dead matter from which we are separated but rather animated and therefore full of *anima* or soul. The cosmos, and particularly the planets in this worldview, are enchanted the way they might be to a poet. This is easily demonstrated in the difference between how an astronomer and an astrologer observe the planets. While both study the same objects, the astronomer is interested in mass, velocity, chemistry, orbital periods, age, and so forth and the astrologer is interested in the poetic meaning of the planets. Archetypal astrologers in particular say that the planets are heavenly representations of archetypal principles. Venus, *Goddess of Beauty and Love,* is certainly not limited to human love and beauty; Venus is just as alive in a chocolate mousse as she is in a passionate kiss. There is always a cultural and historical context to the expression of the archetype, but our readiness to have the experience is universal. If you fall in love in Eastern Ecuador or Western Wales, the experience is remarkably similar and age does not matter either. Your inner Venus is at work here. When you fall in love, Venus takes over your entire inner play. For a while, she becomes the lead character. Similarly, when you become enraged and see red, you step into Mars and he takes over the stage.

The second postulate is based on the philosophical idea of universalism. In astrology there is no separateness. We are not separate from the cosmos or from anything else for that matter. We are one with everything. If this is true then we are part of the planets and the planets are part of us. The ancient doctrine for this was *As Above, So Below.* Jung's concepts of *anima mundi* and the collective unconscious point in this direction in their universality.

The following is a description of the process I apply when using the theatrical metaphor in practice. Much like psychotherapy, astrology is mostly an art form. There is only so much you can learn and then it becomes a matter of intuition, creativity, and chemistry in relating with the client. This worries those who would like to quantify astrology or have it become more "respectable" by the standards of established academia. I find myself too busy with clients who have real-world issues and who appear to benefit from this work, to worry about respectability. Results matter to me more than anything else. I practice archetypal astrology as a helping profession. However we get there—as long as no one gets hurt along the way—is acceptable to me. This is also what I teach my students.

Only after you have entered my practice do I look at your horoscope. I do zero preparations. I used to prepare many supplemental calculations and charts but for the last decade or so I do not look at the horoscope until the client is either in front of me or they have called me on the telephone. There is a huge flow of information that streams through my mind when I see a chart and this is true for most experienced astrologers. Astrology is a symbolic language, like music. To the untrained eye a chart is a mass of lines and glyphs and squiggles on a page, beautiful perhaps but meaningless. If you don't know how to read music and someone hands you Beethoven's Fifth as sheet music you would never grasp the vastness of what you were holding. Every chart I see feels like a symphony to me. I don't prepare because once I look at a chart I see a massive amount of imagery and information that I don't want to lose without first having shared it with my client.

First, I want you to know what is going on in your play. I want you to know who amongst your actors is kissing whom, who is slapping whom, and who is stabbing whom. Just like in a theatrical play I find this out by studying the *relationships* between the actors. There is an astrological technique for this. Getting to know the actors is the first layer in understanding the horoscope. The relationships between them represents the second layer.

Then, the players are also wearing certain outfits and this

changes their behavior. The same way that a person behaves differently if she is wearing a party dress or a night shirt, so by inference this is true of your inner characters as well. We can read this third layer of the horoscope by noting which *sign* a planet is in. In the sky the signs are the background constellations of the Zodiac against which we see the movement of the planets. Here is a practical example. Mars, as we saw above, is the Warrior Lord. This means your Mars will tell us how you might respond if someone held you up in a dark alley at knifepoint. Mars in Aries (Mars dressed as a warrior) would want to fight. Mars in Gemini (Mars dressed as a trickster) would try trickery or to talk his way out of the situation. Mars in Scorpio (Mars showing a gang affiliation tattoo on his arm) would hand over his wallet but remember the mugger's face so that he could track him down later. We see that the sign that a planet is in modifies the behavior of that planet. Keep in mind that we are referring to the martial or Mars part of a person here, not the person as a whole. This is archetypal thinking. We are peopled with these ten characters inside and whatever the situation, the appropriate actor will step forward, instinctively and instantly. This thinking also means that we can actively go and find a character in a person's play if we need help with something. For instance, if someone has a drinking problem and wants help with that, we would go to the most stable character on the stage and see how we could boost the effectiveness of that character in the play by giving him or her a more significant role.

Finally, we also divide the stage into twelve *houses*. This represents the fourth layer of understanding the horoscope. Each planet/actor will show up in one of these twelve segments that represent twelve areas of life. That segment then describes the most natural place that you would express that planet in. Again using Mars as an example, Mars in the 10th house of one's career could mean someone who fights for a living, such as a soldier or a boxer, or even a lawyer who battles for causes in the courtroom. Mars in the 7th house of the partner is more inclined to pick a feisty mate and needs to squabble and fight with a significant other much of the time.

What we recognize is a great complexity in every horoscope.

Once you combine all the possibilities given by the four layers it is easy to get lost in the details, quickly making the interpretation meaningless for the client. The art of astrology is in the synthesis. It is in seeing patterns and themes, what a person is "mostly." Sometimes a theme is so overwhelming that seeing it and mentioning it to the client can bring tears. There are few things in the therapeutic process as powerful as being genuinely *seen*. After 36 years of talking to thousands of people in my practice, the one thing I know for sure is that when a person walks away from an astrological reading having been truly seen, then the client and I have been in a *temenos,* or sacred space, and something magical has happened. I think of Marie-Louise von Franz's metaphorical notion of "getting into the bathtub with your patients" if one wants to be effective in the healing process. Certainly this applies in these moments.

Most interesting to me are the oxymorons in a chart, contradictions that don't make sense at first. I have called this the *Jumbo Shrimp Phenomenon*. Most charts have these and the longer I practice astrology the more I look for these. I find that they define a person at their core. If I want to go deeper I need to recognize and honor this inner conflict that the person before me embodies. Like a giant blocking the way in a fairy tale, this Jumbo Shrimp will also be in the way of any subtler work that we may want to undertake. An example of such an oxymoron is someone who has a strong need to be invisible and private and at the same time a strong desire to constantly push themselves into the public's eye. This might manifest in such a manner that they keep shouting to the world, "Hello everybody, I am this very private person!" We can easily imagine how living with this could be difficult. On the other hand, being seen and recognized for the dynamic energy that this carries is hugely therapeutic and this becomes the starting point for where to go next. We can now discuss what other roles the pushy actor can also play and what parts the shy character will remain comfortable with—all in context of the client's real life, of course.

The giant on the path is a helpful metaphor to understanding our lives. We tend to get caught up in the same stories and issues until we confront them in some way and learn to put our arm around these characters and walk with them as we go forward. In order to do this we need to imagine them as archetypal and not as literal and this is where archetypal astrology can be extremely helpful. Let's say a client enters the consulting room and presents with one or (several) of the following stories: He has always felt rejected by his mother; he feels cold and can't express his feelings; he doesn't want children and his partner does; he suffers from severe claustrophobia, and so on. The astute astrologer will recognize that all these inner pains are based on the same astrological pattern: a Moon-Saturn tension.

In my own practice I will often ask my client to hold out her left hand, with the open surface parallel to the floor. Then I tell her that everyone I have ever met has a pile of crap on their hand, including me. How we deal with this crap (and sometimes I use a more descriptive word) is the key. One of my great teachers, Dave Dobson, once told me that if you have a pile of crap and stir it up, it just stinks. We are not ignoring the stinking issues. By recognizing the astrological pattern that created this crap—here we are calling it Saturn/Moon—we are acknowledging it. We are also choosing not to stir it up. I leave that work to therapists. I am not against analyzing the past and stirring up history; there is certainly some value in that. The issue is that so many of my clients have gotten stuck in that model and never found a way to move on. "Blame psychology" is rampant and alive and, as Hillman and Ventura addressed eloquently in *We've Had a Hundred Years of Psychotherapy—And the World's Getting Worse* (1992) we need to find a better way in the helping professions.

I now ask my clients to hold out their right hand. We begin the process of imagining what Saturn/Moon could be if *they* could decide. I tell them that there are as many ways to live Saturn/Moon as there are people in the world. These are archetypes that are particularly strong in them and they are called to find ways to live them well. An example of this would be to get involved in housing for the poor (Saturn rules architecture and construction and the Moon rules shelter and protection). A Saturn/Moon person would also make a very fair judge because they would not be swayed by emotionality. By moving the focus away from the crappy history we know about an archetype and reimagining it in a new form, we are still honoring that archetypal pattern within us and therefore we are not in denial of who we are. This is a very specific therapeutic option and extraordinarily effective. In the end what applies here is the axiom that *You Do The Gods or The Gods Do You*. Astrology's gift is that we have a tool to find out how to do the gods well.

In every discussion about astrology the issue of the planets' influence on our free will is at least at the perimeter of such conversations. The word "influence" itself comes from the medieval Latin *influentia* which means *emanation of power from the stars*. The root of the word is *in + fluere* to *flow in*. I prefer to turn this imagery on its head and imagine the flow of the characters within each one of us, all the time. This is what influences us for sure, unseen only if we don't pay attention. These inner archetypes, a constant reflection of their heavenly counterparts, are influencing us indeed by acting out their roles. They are the stuff that we are made of. This is an archetypal view of our inner life as opposed to feeling victimized by power emanating from the sky. I also do not believe that we have total free will and can do whatever we want or be anything we want to be. If you are 4' 7" tall you will simply never be the best basketball player. However you may become an excellent jockey. If you are 7' 2" tall, you will never become the best jockey but you might do very well playing basketball. In my practice my focus is to help people find out where the talents are that they may not have discovered yet and what archetypal stories give them a sense of knowing what, despite them not wanting to, they *must* live out. Jung once said astutely: *"Free will is the ability to do gladly that which I must do."*

If we go back to our sheet music metaphor we can use it to think about free will as well. The same piece of music, say Beethoven's Fifth Symphony can by played in remarkably different ways. If you go to YouTube you will find electric guitar versions, disco versions, pop versions, single piano versions, and of course full orchestral symphonic versions. What they all have in common is that we recognize the music immediately. The position of the notes on the sheet makes the music universal and gives it form, rhythm, and structure. This would be akin to the positions of the planets in our horoscope. We have the free will to play with this structure and with these characters in any way we wish. But the actors and their positions are given, so the type of song or play, the recognizable music we will make, is given at birth.

In conclusion, I can attribute the growing interest in archetypal astrology to this: in a world where, even in the helping professions, we are increasingly distanced from enchantment, my clients want to be reimagined in a world that is rich with imagery, metaphor, poetry, mythology, fairytales, and archetypes. If my clients can find their own story and take it out to a larger world in a meaningful way, then something has happened that has been worth our time together.

References

Hillman, J. & Ventura, M. (1992). *We've had a hundred years of psychotherapy—and the world's getting worse.* San Francisco, CA: HarperSanFrancisco.

FROM ATTIC, TO BASEMENT
AND IN BETWEEN

Safron Rossi

Between 2008 and 2010 I was invited three times to James Hillman and Margot McLean's home in Thompson, Connecticut to sort and gather James' work and bring it to Opus Archives and Research Center, the home of his collection. Attending to his work alongside him, he referred to me in one of his infamous faxes as a "cool hand." As steward, two kinds of work was required—the first was to listen to the stories that a stack of papers, a box of notes and ideas, would evoke. This was the work of attending to what presented itself. And there was an understanding that it was important to not always respond to these stories or reveries in a manner which sought to capture, inscribe, memorize, fix them into some indelible form that would live on forever alongside the paper bodies. There is a trust in the archiving process that takes places in the present moment, and is equally as important as the trust ensured in the process of preserving and caring for the collection once it is brought to its next home. This trust requires the second kind of work—taking notes and inventorying, organizing papers and boxes, carefully handling and packing the material for shipment.

James tended his work as though it were a blessing, a necessary blessing, and something that required love. And this was clear by the way he attended to it—he knew what everything was, remembered its providence or significance on the turn of a dime, and he was very organized. Well, mostly organized. On one visit his desk had been swallowed up by a body of papers which "continue to

71

proliferate like fruit flies since you last visited" he said, and required discernment and daily attendance. Sitting in his office and working with him on taming the desk, though arduous and requiring patience because it was everything he was currently working on and each scrap of paper needed to be handled with great attention, was an honor.

James' grace and thoughtfulness in relation to his work was mirrored in what he put aside for the archives and why. These last few years James was working on the *Uniform Edition* so he was reviewing what he had previously written, making minor revisions, and organizing the ideas and essays into the thematic volumes. So as he completed one of those themes, "Mythic Figures" for example, he would let those sheaves of notes, edited essays, and references, go. It seemed a conscious unraveling of his ownership to his own history. And it was a mindful choosing of what would persist after he died—the ideas, the paper trails, the flashes of insight caught on the back of an airline ticket stub. James, Margot, and I spent a lot of time talking about the various projects that could be taken up in his collection because it was important to them that the work carry on. It was all about his work, and his generosity in that regard is clear as reflected in his voluminous collection in the archives. The intention of this whole wild process of mindfully choosing what persists after one dies, James and Margot's vision of his collection, is based on the importance of his legacy rather than on the personal ephemera that inevitably gathers in every life. James chose to withhold, if that is the right word, little except what was very personal. That was his way: he was not interested in personal biography but in the life of the work—his own and those of his colleagues.

The Attic

A good deal of time was spent in the attic. Alighting to the third floor, up the winding staircase and past the bookshelves that held copies of James' books, first editions and reprints, the door to the attic opened onto a large space wherein Tupperware boxes of various sizes and colors were stacked. Some of them contained the library of books used for *A Terrible Love of War* (2004), others were filled with old papers, letters, and memorabilia, business documents for Spring Publications, family photographs, notebooks from his Zurich University days. Along the center aisle of the attic were tables with stacks of papers primed and ready to look through and there were even more bookshelves. Here were copies of all the books James had published at Spring, foreign translations of his work, and duplicates of old issues of *Spring Journal.* And below the books were yet more shelves that contained those numinous cardboard magazine file boxes each labeled with a topic, a project, or an idea that James had worked on at one point and either planned to return to and so needed to be brought down to his office, or were ready for release to the archives. The labels read: "Men's Conferences," "Alchemy," "Cosmology," "Mythic Figures," and contained within them snippets of paper bearing ideas and quotes, references, lists of books to buy, and articles relevant to the theme at hand. By these boxes were stored the red binders that contained the various essays and chapters on alchemy that James had studied through his life. Once through this aisle, the attic opened up again to a larger space and here, at a table with a couple of chairs we would sit down, open one of the boxes Margot pulled over to us, and begin to read, discuss, sort through the delicate paper body of his life.

At times a box would be sorted through quite easily for the items were organized in a coherent way and the material at hand did not require much assessment and deliberation. For example there was a cache of boxes that we labeled "Jungiana" and the items included photographs, manuscripts, letters, and publications that all related to James' time in Zurich at the Institute. There was a collection of maybe a dozen photographic portraits of Jung, one of Toni Wolff, as well as a group photo taken from a party at the Jung Institute in 1954 with Jung and a bevy of people all around him obviously have a grand old time. Memorabilia or perhaps a future research project, it was not always easy to tell the reasoning behind such unexpected finds.

James kept many manuscripts by others because of their significance—whether because they were by brilliant authors and colleagues, deep explorations of a theme, or of historical value. One example that combined all of these reasons was a selection of essays, some possibly unpublished, by Adolf Portmann, whom James called one of the founding figures of archetypal psychology. He talked passionately about the necessity of Portmann's work being translated and published. In these moments the foundational stones of archetypal psychology and his work were literally present, in his memory and in our hands. Here, in Portmann, in Corbin, was the importance of the work and its legacy not of psychology itself but of imagination and soul. James was able to share his desire for them to live on by saving these items and entrusting them to us at Opus.

Other pieces found, and often they surprised him, included a collection of essays published in German that had, among other things, a piece on palmistry and Jung's palms in particular. Strange and curious pieces, items that he knew were important and so held onto, and which now live alongside the rest of his collection at Opus. He also had manuscripts by friends, colleagues, and individuals sent for review, feedback, consideration for possible publication at Spring. These stacks of papers would excite a spark—an example being a manuscript on Mars in the astrological tradition, which though he didn't publish it, intrigued him for having been written by a woman.

And then there were other times, when we were sifting through boxes of themes and ideas, wherein James would sit back, shift the papers on his lap, and Saturn was felt to be very close. "So much to write about, so much unfinished" he said. "Not enough time." In these moments the impact of this process was felt the nearest, the heaviest—and these were quiet moments. Sitting and being present to the time that had passed. Wondering how and why the eros had abandoned a project and never really returned in a way so to have been picked up again, and would not be now, at least not by his hand. And yet the longing, the desire to write on, think further was right there, fierce and bright. All these threads, these loose ends, were, are, inevitable.

And so he let those paper bodies cracking with potential and tasting of times gone by, go. He released them so to keep working on what was at hand—his clarity and focus resolved even after these twilight moments that held possibility, the future, the past, all that could be and was. During one of these visits he had just completed the *Uniform Edition* on alchemy—and the other volumes and essays were beginning to organize themselves in their magazine boxes that I would bring down from the attic, re-label, and place in an easily accessible areas of his office—"Philosophical Thought," "Animals," "City," "Image," "Pathology." And others came down to the first floor into the staging and packing area, finished stories and loose ends alike— "Mythic Figures," "Alchemy," "Jungiana," other people's manuscripts, correspondence, slides, book lists, lecture notes. . . a hundred threads.

Basement

For those three years his work arrived in subsequent waves and now reside in the "stacks" which is how we refer to the rooms in the basement where the archival collections are stored. The Hillman Collection numbers 154 boxes in our database, and the items received over these past few years totals roughly 40 or so additional archival boxes that have not yet been included into the database but which we have volunteers currently helping us input. These 200 boxes range from 1960 to 1999, so nearly 40 years of James' work is with us today—and this will increase over the next couple of years when his post-2000 work comes to us, thereby reflecting over 50 years of his life of work, gathered together under the roof of Opus which is located on the campuses of Pacifica Graduate Institute. Imagine that for each book he wrote there are at least two, sometimes four, archival boxes that contain the whole process of that book from notes to drafts to correspondence.

In the archives there are rows of grey archival boxes patch-worked with Post-it notes indicating the inclusion of these new pieces belonging with those previously placed at home here. A complex weaving of new threads amidst those that began the tapestry of his collection. This is one aspect of what an archive does—preserving what has been entrusted from a life of service to, and love of, ideas, creativity, passion, and discipline. And this is where we find ourselves when we are in the archives—down in the basement, below ground in the catacombs, in the imaginal vault of history. That is to say, in the archetypal field of the Senex. Hillman (1967/2005) writes, "The Senex is itself a god, a universal reality whose ontological power is expressed in nature and culture and the human psyche. As natural, cultural and psychic processes mature, gain order, consolidate and wither, we witness the specific formative effects of the Senex" (p. 251). An archive and the paper bodies that make up the archival body in relationship to the processes that created them are the products of this maturation process. Upon entering the archival field, the formative effects of Senex are honored in all their glory and the paper body of a life is ordered and consolidated and can be seen as the ultimate symbol of maturity, accomplishment, and completion. So in the archives we serve Saturn, the great king and ruler, the elder, the cantankerous and secretive hermit.

Enclosing time in the vaults and archival boxes, Saturn as god of the archives brings rules, history, discipline, and order. The archival collections at Opus are the roots of the wider community of archetypal and depth psychology, and roots are old, part of the past, echoes of eternity ever running deeper and stronger. Saturn is concerned with tradition, authority, and structure—the authority of archives is found in its Latin meaning, as a variant from the Greek *archeion* meaning governmental building, public office which is from the verb *arkho*, "to begin, rule, govern."

In "Senex and Puer: An Aspect of the Historical and Psychological Present" (1967/2005), Hillman reminds us that Saturn is a god of the harvest imaged through the festival of the Saturnalia, but he adds, "the harvest is a hoard; the ripened end-product and in-gathering" (p. 44)—the end-product of a life is what collects in an archive, and an in-gathering holds together, holds tight so to ensure that "things last through all time" (p. 44). Lasting through all time is the fantasy that drives our work digitizing the collections, creating digital bodies of paper bodies that were created by living bodies. Hillman goes on to say that Saturn's "intellectual qualities include the inspired genius of brooding melancholic, creativity through contemplation" (p. 44). This brooding melancholy and the contemplative creative spark is often what we see descend upon a research visitor when they behold the archives, open a box, and are swallowed up. And it isn't a surprise for us to find that our visitors at times feel overwhelmed and slightly depressed by the experience.

And we have to be honest, there is a sense of death in the archives, the kind that the Senex brings, and this Hillman (1967/2005) writes,

> is the death that comes through perfection and order. It is the death of accomplishment and fulfillment, a death which grows in power within any complex or attitude as that psychological process matures through consciousness into order, becoming habitual and dominant—and therefore unconscious again. Paradoxically, we are least conscious where we are most conscious. (p. 45)

This is the awkward truth Jung had discerned and, as the archives lie below the surface and require twilight vision, we are confronted with this uneasy paradox. The perfection and order of the collections down in the archives is a death and the consciousness that created them has become unconscious in their orderliness—and here lies the danger— the hardening, the dryness, consciousness losing touch with life. And without the folly of life Hillman writes, the Senex "has no wisdom, only knowledge—serious depressing, hoarded in an academic vault or used as power" (p. 48). This is a serious archetypal constellation and I must admit feeling a little fear at times in the face of the hoarding impulse that comes with this territory.

The cure is like to like, and so Senex needs Puer. Puer as "avatar of the psyche's spiritual aspect" (Hillman, 1967/2005, p. 50), aesthetic intuition, insight, and the blossoming of imagination. This Puer blossoming, in relationship to Senex rootedness, is the life that visits the archives, the ideas seeking ground, spirit seeking form and discipline.

And that is what happens when *you* come into the archives—

spinning fantasies of golden treasure and fantastic flights of imagination, you wander through the stacks, through the boxes and pages within, longing for a reflection of your own ideas, an authoritative buttressing of your notions, you are lost, you get lost, not sure where to go but with a glorious idea about where you are going for just around the next box is going to be that very passage that will have everything fall into place in your project, you can feel it. . . you are the spirit, the Puer impulse that the Senex archives needs so to not harden, to not dry out, to stay in touch with life. As a union of the sames, Senex and Puer belong together, seek one another, and when they unite knowledge becomes wisdom, and spirit and insight find reflection and form.

In Between

Archives exist in between this union of Senex and Puer. And really, if we look at what makes an archive, it is the ever-constant cycling of these two figures—coming into the archives, becoming a part of the archives, only to return again and infuse the archives with questions and spirited life, which will then become yet another part of the archives. An urobouric image like Opus' logo of the circle with two tails—the inflowing of ideas, becoming form, and eventually flowing out again. Ultimately, what makes up a life is what makes up Opus.

As stewards, our mission at Opus is to preserve, develop, and extend to the world the Hillman collection, along with the other eight scholars whose work we care for. This threefold mission is mirrored in our programs that include offering scholarships, research grants, educational programs, community events, and research access to the collections, both physically and digitally. And yet while our mission and programs reveal all that we do, there is still a palpable mystique to the archives; this place necessarily constellates a sense of mystery and has a concealed aspect that serves Senex well. So here are some images to bring the mysterious quality to a place where our work can be felt. To preserve the work is to attend to the paper bodies and organize the work so that the breadth of a collection is cohesive, ordering the threads so to mirror the end product of an intellect's life but at the same time to lead to unexpected finds, connections that exist beyond simply by the boxes being placed alongside one another.

We also preserve the work by digitizing it because in the end no amount of proper storage, air conditioning, and humidity control will allow these pieces to last forever. We have to remember that they are paper bodies and like all bodies they will eventually disintegrate, fall apart. So we dance with Hermes, a constant puer companion, and capture the audio lecture, pictures and slides, handwritten notes in a digital image. All the while knowing over time these formats too will have to change, and the digital body will transform.

Our second charge is to develop the collections, and while this does include bringing new collections in over time, I want to focus more on the aspect of development that has to do with deepening, not just growing. To develop James' work means refining the catalogue of what we have and eventually developing a sophistication in our database that will allow us to cross reference all the places, all the boxes and lectures or drafts therein around a theme, or a figure. Imagine the depth of association and connection in being able to locate throughout James' collection all the places he quoted Plotinus, or mentioned Zeus, or Demeter. This deepening development would allow us to move from the universal view of James' paper body and into the particular. We would move from seeing Pan across ten boxes and find him on one snippet of paper, reflected in one of James' thoughts.

And finally extending the collections into the world is making them available to more schools, scholars, students, artists, and writers. Opus seeks to support interdisciplinary dialogue as it informs critical current issues in the fields of the Humanities, the Arts, Cultural and Civic Life, Education, Social Justice, the Environment, and Health and Healing. All these themes we find reflected in James' work because these themes are what constitute our lives, individually and collectively.

Educating our community and the wider culture to the treasures that we have and the importance of the work that lies therein is part of our vision and mission. I often refer to Opus as a "living archive" because these treasures *are* alive in that they offer among many things wisdom, curiosity, shifts in perspectives, challenges and confirmations to the questions that we seek in our own work to circumscribe answers to, articulate, complicate, think on and go further, deeper.

It takes a community to support Opus' work of caring for and making available the legacy of our elders and our ancestors, for us now and future generations. James Hillman has become our ancestor, one of the great men of the past he himself honored and this passage from elder to ancestor is what we are now paying tribute to. And as a community we are honored and challenged to attend, care, and give, in order to sustain his legacy.

I have one last story to share from a woman who had volunteered at the newly created archives in the early 90's when Joseph Campbell's library arrived at Opus. In the midst of our conversation she shared an extraordinary memory and kindly gave me permission to share it with you today. She was sitting in the Campbell Library on Pacifica's Lambert Road campus and the door was open. Suddenly James appeared in the doorway, backlit. He was vivid, she said, there with his smile and warmth. He took a breath and in his rich voice said, "Ah, the heart of the place."

References

Hillman, J. (2004). *A terrible love of war*. New York, NY: Penguin.
Hillman, J. (2005). Senex and puer: An aspect of the historical and psychological present. In G. Slater (Ed.), *Senex & puer: Uniform edition of the writings of James Hillman* (Vol. 3, pp. 30-70). Putnam, CT: Spring. (Original work published 1967)

"DEAR JAMES": THE ACADEMIC CRUSH AND THE ARC OF INFLUENCE

Jennifer Leigh Selig

Dear James,

My name is Jennifer Selig, and I'm a Pacifica person, on the faculty since 2005, currently serving as the creator and program chair of the Depth Psychology M.A./Ph.D. degree with an emphasis in Jungian and Archetypal Studies. You were to have spoken before my students last Thursday evening, 40 students in their first year of studying Jungian and archetypal psychology, a very committed and enthusiastic bunch, some of whom are very familiar with your work, others new to it, but all passionately looking forward to their studies, driven by their desire to bring this work out into the world.

He was to have spoken, but he was dying. The synchronicity was not lost on me, that as he was dying, an academic program dedicated in large part to the legacy of his work was birthing, borning. As he was slipping past twilight darkness on the East Coast into his own midnight hour, it was early morning on the West Coast. The ouroboros of time was bending into an arc in preparation for a taste of its own tail.

It occurred to me then that though I've introduced you to groups of students in previous years when I was chair of the Depth Psychology program, I've never spoken more than a few words to you personally, and certainly never shared any bit of my journey to Pacifica with you.

This was disingenuous of me, and cowardly. It didn't *just* occur to me that I hadn't spoken to him much. I acutely and consciously avoided him at all accounts and at all costs. I was always cowardly when it came to this man, intimidated by his intellectual power, and the Martial force of his character. I could listen to him forever, but I couldn't entertain talking to him for a minute.

Now that he's gone, I will tell you what I couldn't tell him. He lived on Pacifica's Ladera campus for several months at a time each spring. On one such spring morning, I arrived on campus to defend my doctoral dissertation. I was nervous, as anyone would be, but when I saw him coming down the stairs into the parking lot, I got back into my car and started the engine and almost drove away. The thought of him being in the room *listening to me* was terrifying. Of course, he wouldn't be listening to me because I would be paralyzed, unable to speak. I could have traded a Ph.D. for an A.B.D. (All But Dissertation) if it meant avoiding that anxiety.

It is because of you, if you'll forgive me for being so linear and causal. . .

He won't. I know he hates simple causality. "Why" we do anything is unknowable and overdetermined, he would say. I know this. I ask for forgiveness, hoping he'll understand that I'm making a rhetorical point.

. . . that I came to Pacifica as a student in 1998. Though many students find their way to us because of an encounter with Memories, Dreams, Reflections, *or because of the Joseph Campbell connection, it was when I heard that you had selected Pacifica to house your archives that I knew I must come.*

I'm not entirely sure this is historically accurate, but I know that it's psychologically true. I know of all people, he would appreciate the difference and allow me the truth of my own fiction.

Speaking of fiction, that's what it would have felt like then if you told me that one day I would be on the faculty of Pacifica, and my office would be next to the large storage closet that was temporarily housing the Hillman papers until the permanent archival space was finished. One night, when no one else was in the building, I tried my key in the door of the archives. It opened. I went in. I touched his papers, his letters, scraps of napkins with notes on them. I only stayed five minutes. It was too overwhelming. I was like Semele, one of the many admirers of Zeus, but I knew better than to ask to see my god in all of his glory—I sensed that if I stayed longer, I would be consumed by lightening-ignited flames.

It was We've Had a Hundred Years of Psychotherapy—And the World's Getting Worse *that hooked me. It was an introduction to your thinking that was both accessible and profound, and I nearly threw out my neck nodding with affirmation at the content. Yes, yes, and YES! I bought more of your books, pouring through them as one does with work that is both strange and familiar. It was epiphany, James, reading your work then. It remains so today.*

Look at me, gushing. My academic crush on him continues, a decade and a half later. This letter is slightly embarrassing and highly revealing of my own psychology. I should probably crumple it up and go lie down on a therapist's couch.

I'll never forget the first day of my courses on the Lambert campus. It was lunch, and I was sitting around the table with my new cohort members. We were talking about your work, and I stepped out of the conversation for a moment and said to myself, "I can't believe I'm sitting around a table with people who know James Hillman's work. I can't believe I'm having a conversation about this." It was a moment of pure joy and wonder coupled with affirmation.

I do know how ridiculous this will sound to the 99% of the world who do not worship at the altar of intellectual gods. This is starting to sound like a schoolgirl fan letter to Justin Bieber.

Thirteen years later, and I found myself tonight sitting around the dinner table with my colleagues, some of whom are your dear friends—Robert Romanyshyn, Ginette Paris, Dennis Slattery—and we're having a conversation about your life and work, and I feel that same feeling, that same sense of blessing, of grace, of being in the right place. And wonder—in addition to being a student of your work, I am now one who is bringing your work to students, hopefully in ways that are both accessible and profound.

Sitting there with his friends, I felt a form of generation envy. I felt like mine was the generation *after* the great generation. I could bring their generation's work to my students, but who are the intellectual gods of my generation? Who among my generation will steer the boat, will chart the course, will set students a'sail on the arc of influence?

I felt another emotion at that dinner table—sadness. It was like being told about a great party that you just missed. I envied them their stories of him, flesh and blood and bones, humor and drama and trauma, food and wine and animals, walking and talking and dancing.

I had his books. None signed, because I was too scared.

You would not recognize my face if you were to speak these words to you in person. Every occasion I was around you, I was small, too tucked inside of my own complexes to reach out and tell you what your work has meant to me, what your work does mean to me. This is my regret, this being so impossibly human that I couldn't honor where honor was due, couldn't say this into your piercing brown eyes, which always seemed to me blue.

But this is not true. Or rather, only part of it is true, that I was being "impossibly human" and thus, afraid of him. It is also true that I was not being true to myself in being so small around him. I was not honoring my own largeness.

This is what I know now, truly know in the intervening months-turned-year after his death. He spoke about how our souls, indeed all the souls in the *anima mundi*, have their own particular display. I made a fundamental error in thinking that to be a truly great educator, I needed to be *great like him*. This is an error, because though it is true that I will never be a great intellectual like him, *educating through the fiery intellect is only one way to educate*. There are other ways, and dare I say, ways in which I might be stronger than him. He served his gods, and I serve mine, as you serve yours. To be a great archetypalist means to notice our own particular display, and to notice the display of others. Not to *compare*, but to *contrast*. I was scared of him because I wasn't him. I did not have his Martial energy, but I needed to learn "to fight the hardest battle which any human being can fight and never stop fighting," according to poet e. e. cummings—*to be nobody but myself.* To teach my students not to be him, not to be me, but to be *nobody but themselves.*

And with this realization, and only now, do I earn these final lines of my letter to him.

> *Still, at Pacifica, I carry out my commitment to you.*
> *Your student,*
> *Jennifer*

I held the envelope to my heart for a brief moment before I sent it off. Of course, I would never expect and could never imagine a reply, but weeks later, one arrived in my email box. The subject line read *From James Hillman as dictated to Margot.* I didn't open it right away. After all, it took me 15 years to write my academic love letter to him; how could I be expected to open any reply of his anytime soon, and without shaking. This shocked my partner who found the waiting disrespectful, but I knew it was not. The ouroboros takes her time. She slowly opens her mouth for her tail.

Then one day, hunger struck, and I was ready to open completely.

Dear Jennifer,

The first paragraph was lovely, pure acknowledgment of my letter and my devotion to *our common work.* The *our* thrilled me inordinately. Not his, not mine, but *ours,* I thought. The academic crush becomes the alchemical marriage; *we,* James and I, devoted to *our common work.*

The second paragraph switched tone.

I have one critique.

Critique? Of personal fanmail?

At the end of your first paragraph, you write the phrase "driven by their desire to bring this work out into the world." The alchemists often warned against the reddening coming too fast. Jung's Red Book *shows the importance of the investigations altogether apart from utility or wider understanding. The urge toward the world needs analysis. Else you become a missionary.*

What? But wait, I thought. Isn't the urge toward the world the very thing he was suggesting in the very first book of his I read? *We've Had a Hundred Years of Psychotherapy and the World's Getting Worse*—isn't the urge toward the world part of what will help the world get better instead? I thought he said. . .

Suddenly, I realized something. He was still teaching me. He was still confounding me, still confronting me, still challenging me, still doing and undoing anything, everything he has said. He was still making me think and making me feel. I am ever and always his student for life.

And after his death, I received an email from one of my

students who wanted to run a paper topic by me, and who lightly, at the very end, confessed to having an academic crush on me and coming to Pacifica because of me. I smiled. I am no James Hillman. I will never strike such fear in the hearts of my students or become anyone's intellectual god. But I am here because of him, and someone is here because of me. The ouroboros bites his tail. The arc of influence comes full circle, complete.

THE ARCHETYPAL "METHOD": REFLECTIONS ON HILLMAN'S APPROACH TO PSYCHOLOGICAL PHENOMENA

Glen Slater

Faced with a rich and extensively body of writings and now the absence of their author, we have over the coming years both the opportunity and the responsibility to *foster the tone* for engaging the archetypal psychology of James Hillman. And whereas this may be both an inspiring and a weighty task, we should recall the enormously colorful and diverse array of fields and regions in which Hillman's work has taken root. No doubt there will flourish multiple interpretations and applications of this psychology, befitting its polytheistic bearing and the panoply of perspectives Hillman drew upon and addressed. Beside depth psychology, archetypal theory has entered ecopsychology, the literary and visual arts, architecture, religious studies, cultural criticism, social justice, and communications. This interest in applying Hillman's ideas in different ways to different aspects of human endeavor will certainly prevent codified renderings. However, those of us who have come into his work through our Jungian psychological training and/or the practice of psychotherapy will have a more pivotal role to play in the interpretation and distillation of archetypal thought, involving a more extensive study of his ideas and a more deliberate consideration of what he was doing and how he was doing it. It's in this spirit that I wish to make a preliminary foray into the question of Hillman's *method*.

Fostering a fitting tone requires awareness of the most salient roots of his work, so we see not only its fruitful outcomes but can appreciate and draw upon its deeper sources. The question of method means discerning critical characteristics of his approach, exploring whether these characteristics can be raised to the level of principles, and considering the consistency of their presence. We also need to cultivate a sense of where his approach grows out of Jung's. Despite Hillman's challenge to major parts of Jung's opus, and even more so to some of its interpreters, he remained a Jungian, never losing sight of the archetypal ground of the psyche Jung's work established, nor the vivid phenomenology of psychic reality that infused the master's approach. Hillman's work assumes the archetypal patterns of psychological life and takes their imagistic and mythic expression as axiomatic. This sets the governing idea and the basic path of inquiry: according to Hillman, all significant displays of psychological life may be understood by tracing "the *epistrophé* or reversion through likeness of an event to its mythical pattern," or an "archetypal sensitivity that all things belong to myth" (1997, p. 47).

The twist Hillman brings to this starting point is a more radical embrace of Jung's insight that there's no Archimedean point outside of the psyche from which to conduct psychological study. We study the psyche by means of the psyche. Whereas Jung had embraced this understanding with his study of psychological types and their influence on theorizing—acknowledging all psychologies reflected the subjectivity of their theorists and the psyche surrounded us on all sides—he often reverted to the stance of an empiricist capable of objective observation. But Hillman, moving from the archetypal ground of the psyche and its essential forms of fantasy and image, more fully embraced the idea that these "universals" dominate our "modes of apprehension" (Jung, 1960, p. 137) and are thus inseparable from both our perceptions and our ideas. *Our* ideas are, at the end of the day, not ours at all, but belong to the gods. Theories and their associated research methods also display archetypal forms, which require depth psychologists to become aware, not only of the object of their study but the means by which the study is conducted and the phenomenon apprehended. We don't just seek an understanding of the gods at work—we must also see the gods at work in our understanding. This is what he meant by "applying psychology to psychology" (Hillman, 1972, p. 40). And given that our psychologies and worldviews dictate the way we imagine into lived experience, we also need to subject our ideas to deeper consideration, looking for the mythic and archetypal patterns at work therein—most often quite unconsciously. In life and in psychology, we're continually reenacting mythical dramas, a deeper awareness of which expands our sense of soul and allows greater reflexivity.

Searching for archetypal patterns and neglected cultural-historical backgrounds within theories is what Hillman came to call "a therapy of ideas," the most powerful application of which is on display in his two major works, *The Myth of Analysis* (1972) and *Re-Visioning Psychology* (1975), where he subjects first the analytical psychology of Jung and then psychology in general to archetypal scrutiny, locating the mythic reversions at work therein, creating openings for new ways of envisioning the psyche and its proclivities. For example, in the first of these works, he takes three largely rarified and abstract concepts—transference, the unconscious, and neurosis—and he reverts the essence of these "pillars" of the analytical tradition to Eros, the imaginal, and the appearance of Dionysos (1972, p. 8), providing pathways to deepen the sense of complexity that resides in each. The aim is to raise our awareness, but for Hillman the *kind* of awareness resulting from the process is what matters. Myth, metaphor, and a more poetic language cultivate the imagination, joining past and present, preserving the feeling of fathomless depth that can only be called soulful. Whereas, he argued, analytical, Apollonian language belongs to the bright lights and distancing stance of science and medicine, reinforcing the rationalism the depth approach is supposed to move us beyond.

Hillman does not, therefore, abandon the fundamental imperative of all depth psychology—to make what is unconscious more conscious. He just doesn't wish to draw the depths up into the light of consciousness so much as to adapt the conscious mind to the depths. Here, the *way* one hosts, comprehends, and insights a given phenomenon or event is also how meaning and significance is generated. In this manner, soul, that quality of being he placed at the center of his work, is not so much the result of his psychological method as it is an implication of it. Soul is generated by being psychological, by practicing a psychology befitting psyche. This is what we must now explore.

Cautions

The term "method" refers to a mode of inquiry: how one goes about investigating or understanding something; the procedure employed in such investigation. More specifically, it indicates the consistency and level of conscious design in such inquiry, conveyed by adjectives like "systematic," "orderly," and "habitual." It implies "discipline" and "technique." Such terms pepper the dictionary definition of "method" (Merriam-Webster online), which is also shorthand for the more elaborate term "methodology"—adding the *logos* that implies a significant degree of analysis and scrutiny of the mode of inquiry, translated into particular steps and principles.

I remind us of these understandings to convey just how cautious we need to be applying a term like method to the work of James Hillman, whose approach to psychological life was notoriously and determinedly *un*systematic, *dis*orderly, and anything but habitual. It's certainly short on descriptions of procedures and techniques. His emphasis on polymorphic styles of rhetoric and engagement gives rise to an understandable resistance to the question of method; each topic requires a different approach based on its differing archetypal background. Another aspect of this resistance relates to something very much at the heart of Hillman's understanding of the psyche. To hijack Casey's well known statement on images: for Hillman, psychology is not so much about what you see, but *the way you see*. Psyche has to do with vision, with imagining. In this vein, psychology is all about how we might best approach the psyche; it's all about the perspective we bring. Thus, in a significant sense, his method pervades his psychology in a way that's hard to extract. A third aspect of this resistance follows the same point: any attempt to extract general principles risks overshadowing the singular quality of his writings, which are topically wide-ranging, expressive of certain moments in the history of the field, and indelibly imprinted with the author's idiosyncrasies. As he admits in the 1992 preface to *Re-Visioning Psychology* (1975), even in a work devoted to moving the focus of psychology beyond the personal, "psychology is always and inescapably confession. Every text reveals the weaver's predilections. . . . Like the carpet, the book is a highly idiosyncratic product" (p. ix). So an emphasis on method can lead us right out of this highly textured fabric; method can be a fantasy of escaping the unique weaving of time and place and person that makes up a depth psychological engagement. Dare I say it: the fantasy of method might even oppose that of soul. To be certain, soul-making and the cultivation of imagination (the goals of archetypal psychology) require something more than method.

With such cautions in mind, I'd like to argue that Hillman *did* employ a method of sorts, though I doubt it's possible to raise this approach to the level of a pervasive *methodology*. For while we do get glimpses of what we might think of as a "logos of method"—that is, careful consideration and description of what he was doing as he was doing it—there's little in Hillman to suggest any project of systematizing this layer of awareness or turning it into a discipline. There are, however, several salient references to method, especially in his earlier work. And if we go back to these, a case can be made for the presence of distinct modes of engaging the psyche that are sustained throughout his writings and prove consistent and pivotal enough to be referenced in terms of method.

Early Reflections on Method

The most transparent and in some ways traditional discussion of method appears in Hillman's first major publication in 1960, *Emotion*. Given this book was generated from his doctoral thesis, the prominence of methodological discussion is not surprising. Yet his discussion here tells us more about the ultimate direction of his approach than we might expect; the essence of Hillman's method appears to be there from the beginning. Whereas his ideas certainly expanded, and the polytheistic emphasis that resides at the heart of the archetypal approach had yet to be articulated, two critical, even defining characteristics of his psychology are in place by the end of this initial major publication. First, he's already doing a psychology of psychology or a *therapy of ideas*. And second, he comes to rest his insights and understandings in images, particularly mythic images, preempting the poetic basis of mind that comes to reside at the heart of his perspective. Despite the fact that this book comes more than a decade before archetypal psychology surfaces as a distinct offshoot of Jungian thought, it sets out key and enduring characteristics of his approach.

Emotion (1960) is an exhaustive consideration of theories of affect. It is, he makes clear from the start, not an investigation into emotions *per se*, but a study that "turn(s) directly to the theories themselves . . . exposing the models of thinking about emotion" (p. 18). It attempts to survey the various and conflicting perspectives on the topic and "bring order out of confusion, agreement out of disagreement" (p. 9). And whereas this quest ends in what he describes as a "condensation" of understandings (p. 287), he nonetheless concludes the work by stating: "Perhaps this is why no matter how thoroughly amplified, the problem of emotion, theory and therapy, remains perennial and its solution ineffable" (p. 289). So we needn't worry that the early Hillman was invested in neat, uncomplicated solutions! Yet it is clear that the focus on *ideas*, on thinking itself as a window into the psyche and as a locale for practicing psychology, begins here.

He states:

Our method, therefore, is a 'therapy' in that going through the work—that continual confrontation with the 'why' of emotion—is an enlargement of comprehension. It is a process of enlightenment which can result in an acceptance, an affirmation even, of emotion, which is precisely what, as said often and again, is required for its development. The prolonged encounter with the problem of emotion is already—by admitting it as a problem—an attempt on the part of consciousness to come to terms with it, which is the first step towards the development of any problem. Or, to put it another way, the circumambulation of this phenomenon has altered our relation to it. (p. 288)

This very early project already sounds like classic Hillman, arguing that the study of *ideas* surrounding a topic—in this case emotion—will take us right to the heart of phenomenon and how it sits in the human psyche. Even more impressive, punctuating the point, he states: "However we put it, *explanatory and therapeutic psychology in regard to emotion are enmeshed with each other*" (1960, p. 287). This entwining of ideas and practice comes some fifteen years before his critique of the tendency to split thought and action, which punctuated the *Re-Visioning Psychology* chapter called "Psychologizing" (1975, pp. 113ff.). There he wrote: "We are used to contrasting idea and action, believing that subjective reflection restricts action, sickling it over with the pale cast of psychological thought. . . . But action and idea are not inherent enemies, and they should not be paired as a contrast" (p. 116). For Hillman, engaging ideas *was* doing psychology, and the failure to examine ideas, especially in psychology, leads to blind, unreflected actions and techniques.

The philosophically astute discussion of research method in this early work also demonstrates what will become a signature trait: adopting those parts of a theory or approach that suit his purpose and leaving other parts behind, feeling little obligation to consistently or systematically adopt the whole. He takes up phenomenology, for example, but goes on to argue that the critical procedure of bracketing out preconceptions and scientific understandings (sometimes called *epoché*) is unworkable if one is to study the full range of ideas, just as the experimental approach, wanting to leave out immediate lived experience and existential reflections, would also fail the test of inclusion. He makes clear that, in their purist forms, the phenomenological and experimental approaches "cancel each other out" (1960, p. 11). Thus while considering traditional research methods, Hillman avoids sitting squarely in any of them, because they can't embrace the full range of reflection, fantasy, and notion associated with the topic. His solution was to adopt a method he calls "amplification."

Buried in this one word is a seed for Hillman's mature thought. In the idea of amplification, of course, we find the whole temper of Jung's synthetic rather than reductive approach to psychic material. But there's more going on here, and it points us straight to what I consider the largely unrecognized core of Hillman's method, namely, a polytheism that reflects not merely the archetypal *basis* of the psyche but the psychologist's *habit of mind, an ability to open a topic up by considering its polyvalent, multifaceted nature.* Hillman's life-long aversion to reductive, monotheistic concepts thus takes root in this first book. Moreover, he backs this move in a clever way, arguing that "since method is a *way of going about things*," and "*about*" is defined as "around the outside; on or towards every side; all around" (1960, p. 22), then the amplification of a complex phenomenon "and those complex theories about that complex state" (p. 21) is a kind of intrinsic, essential—we might even say "archetypal"—form of method.

Hillman qualifies his use of amplification in two directions, referring to *differentiated* amplification and *integrated* amplification. First looking at many aspects, examining a topic from many angles and on many levels, then locating both a critical idea and a fitting image. In *Emotion* (1960) that critical idea is Aristotle's theory of four levels of causality, which both guides the amplificatory process *and* offers a means of integrating the findings. And the integrative image is the *centaur*, half man, half horse. In each instance he's reaching back to origins, to what is timeless in thought and imagination—an archetypal idea and an archetypal image. The summary motif in particular is striking. After first invoking the "dark, unruly horse of the Phaedrus myth" (p. 288) and its desperate charioteer, he moves on to the integrative image:

> Centaurs were said to be able to capture wild bulls which expresses the idea that wilder emotion can be tamed by conscious emotion, or as was said before. . . "only through emotion can emotion be cured." And it was the centaur, mythology tells us, who taught mankind something of the arts of music and medicine—as if to say the origins of healing our emotional malaise are to be found in the union of mind with flesh, of wisdom and passion. . . . Development means a qualitative process of constant relationship approximating to the nature of the centaur, whereby through the harness of reins and chains. "I become the horse and the horse me." (p. 289)

As Dick Russell records in Hillman's biography, one early potential publisher said the book would "set psychology back 300 years" (2013, p. 463). He goes on the quote Scott Becker, who described this as Hillman's "abandon(ment) of conceptual thinking . . . in favor of mythic imagination," quipping that "300 years may have been a gross underestimation" (p. 463). Here already, method, therapy, and theory are tightly interlaced. Put differently, both approach and theory are therapeutic. Soul is not a thing, as he would later describe it, but a perspective, a way of deepening and recovering psychic significance (1975, p. xvi). Ideas and images provide the means of holding psychic phenomena. We come to see that within the term "amplification" resided both a polytheistic approach and the move towards imagination. Yet before we develop this insight further we need to bring in another major aspect of archetypal psychology's method.

The Puer Process

Perhaps Hillman's most revealing statements on this topic concern his approaching psychological material via the *puer eternus*, the archetype of eternal youth. The ground is broken with his 1967 Eranos presentation "Senex and Puer: An Aspect of the Historical and Psychological Present" (Hillman, 2005). The puer orientation toward more spirited insight is at once a deliberate style of thought, an acknowledgment of personal inclination, and an assessment of how depth psychology might best proceed if it is to achieve the goal of soul-making. Hillman many times hinted that his motivation to bring puer life and renewal to senex stasis sprang from his battles with the old guard of Zurich Jungians. The strength of this thread in the archetypal psychology carpet is now confirmed with the publication of the Russell biography, which shows the young James Hillman surrounded and feeling suffocated by older first generation analysts. While this element was to really take hold of Hillman's life in the mid to later sixties, it was a feeling that seemed to follow him from the start of his time in Zurich (he was just 26 when he arrived in 1953). As if to portend the later explosion of this theme, the final section of *Emotion* opens with a quote that reads: "Instead of explanatory hypotheses being treated with the *maximum* skepticism when they are *new*, and the *minimum* when they are *old*, a reversal of this policy might be profitable" (J. H. Woodger as quoted in Hillman, 1960, p. 241). Old and new, senex and puer, begin their face-off.

The markers set out in this initial 1967 paper, and the return to the topic over time are primarily documented in what is now the third volume of the *Uniform Edition* of Hillman's writings (2005), which includes the striking coda on methodology at the end of *The Soul's Code: In Search of Character and Calling* (1996). There he writes of the "archetypal styles of theories" and states:

> Any theory that is affected by the puer will show dashing execution, appeal to the extraordinary, and a show-off aestheticism. It will claim timelessness and universal validity, but forgo the labors of proof. It will have that puer dance in it, will imagine ambitiously and rebel against convention. A puer-inspired theory will also limp among the facts, even collapse when met with the questioning inquiries of so-called reality....

(2005, pp. 312-313)

That is, the position taken up by "the gay-faced king or Saturn figure" (p. 313)—the senex. Hillman continues with a meta-statement on our theme:

> This kind of self-reflection belongs to psychological method. Unlike the methods used by other disciplines when positing their ideas, an archetypal psychology is obliged to show its own mythical premises, how it is begging its first question. . . Because theories are not merely cooked up in the head or induced from cold data, they represent the dramas of myth in conceptual terms, and the drama is played out in arguments over paradigm shifts. (p. 313)

The thirty years that passed between his initial engagement with the topic and this strident statement at the end of his 1996 best-selling work contain several other telling references. In the very first sentence of *The Myth of Analysis* (1972), the first book publication to signal a major reassessment of Jungian theory, Hillman refers to "the problems of method" being worked out in relation to the *puer eternus* (p. 3). Indeed, the book is a reworking of three papers first presented at Eranos in 1966, 1968, and 1969, essentially surrounding his 1967 senex and puer presentation at the same venue. He describes *The Myth of Analysis* as "a companion book" to a then-in-process manuscript on the puer, which never eventuated—at least in the form he had imagined. But in taking on the analytical stance, the language of the clinic and psychopathology, as well as the masculinized knowledge base of the field, the papers put his puer-imbued method to work, revamping depth psychology, working from within the arena of Jungian ideas. "The problems of method" as he called them appear to have been folded into the new perspective he was expounding, soon to be fully realized in his masterwork, *Re-Visioning Psychology* (1975). Clearly the ongoing engagement with puer themes and problems occupies the immediate background of both these revolutionary works. In his 1992 retrospective preface to *Re-Visioning Psychology*, he indicated his need to postpone the work on the key text because of the puer project, which he there described as "a prolonged and still incomplete defense of my traits and behaviors" (1975, p. xiii).

A window into the way the puer-inspired method is at work in these major writings is provided by Hillman's essay, "Notes on Opportunism" (2005), first published in the 1979 *Puer Papers*. In particular, this paper shows how the method is tied to the polytheistic view of the psyche that had become the most prominent theme of his writings. As both the messenger of the gods and a carrier of puer traits, Hermes provides the connective tissue, and also provides a natural, archetypal opening to couch the approach in terms of hermeneutics. As Hillman writes:

> Hermes is the world itself (reminding us of Jung's statement that Mercurius is the god of the unconscious). 'Hermes' is a way of living in the world, a . . . specific kind of consciousness that creates a 'cosmos' . . . in likeness to itself. Each style of consciousness, such as Hermes, regards the world in a self-consistent way, thereby creating world and mankind according to its image. There are not a multiplicity of worlds and mankinds, yet there are many Gods. Thus for the Gods to create after their likenesses, they must be able to use the same world in many manners, creating styles of being and perception so that our one and only world may participate in a shifting realm of many perspectives, at one moment mimetic to Zeus, and the next to Aphrodite or Ares. . . . This variety of divine forms is the first message of Hermes-Mercurius. . . All things provide divine opportunities for the Gods. (pp. 100-101)

He goes on, describing a style of awareness that carries the ability to "see through" the world to the activity of the gods: "The cosmos of one God, via Hermes, suddenly swings open into that of another. We see one viewpoint from that of another. This is Hermes operating in our vision—the God of betweens, keeping us to the world and guiding us out of it at the same instant" (2005, p. 101).

Later, in the same essay, he once again collapses the divide between seeing and living, thought and action: "Opportunism is a way of living the world, creating a Mercurial cosmos" or what he then calls a "puer mercurial cosmos" with a "situationalist ethic" (2005, p. 106). And now he brings the line of inquiry home: "Every human complexity and every psychological complex, perceived from the puer perspective, is a situation serving its own purposes. When perceived in terms of the puer, there is intentionality in all psychic life. Every situation is headed somewhere" (p. 106). Hillman is clearly making the argument that a puer-based method is tantamount to what we could call a hermetic hermeneutic, which allows us to perceive and allow the play of the gods, bearing witness to the archetypal basis of mind.

Having pointed out the prominence of this aspect of Hillman's approach, including its personal claim, we now need to consider it in a broader context. In depth psychology we learn that personal captivation by a problem or theme does not necessarily invite a reduction to biographical factors. Jung's involvement with the problem of religion has obvious biographical moorings, but it would be absurd to reduce his writings on this topic to his pastor father and spiritualist mother, just as we would not wish to reduce Freud's focus on sexuality to his own relational world and neglect the socio-cultural context of his thought. Hillman's involvement with the puer pattern invites the same turn to cultural significance.

Both the movement of his initial 1967 paper on the topic and his psychology as a whole are towards what he calls a "union of sames" (2005, pp. 58ff.). Senex and puer are two faces of one archetypal configuration, which when split results in *only* senex or *only* puer phenomena—either rigid dogma or flighty, untethered rebellion or innovation. Hillman's goal was never "only puer." As such, his championing of the new—the imaginative, fresh, sparky insight—was not at the expense of the old, but was intended to *revision* the old in new ways. And with the return to the Greeks, the Renaissance, and his constant skirmishing with classical Jungian thought, the old was never far away.

In 2000 I wrote a paper critiquing Hillman's emphasis on the puer and archetypal psychology's lack of ownership of its positive senex qualities (Slater, 2000). Upon reading it Hillman pushed back, reminding me of the tireless scholarship, voluminous references, and extensive historical comparisons in the background and often in the actual footnotes to his writings. He was essentially arguing that while the fruits of his psychology may seem flashy and opportunistic, the ideas spring from careful incubation and discipline. My point then was that this disciplined, careful scholarship needs to be made more transparent, and this current discussion is a variation on the same theme. A *method,* aligned with the *puer,* is itself a *senex-et-puer* notion; the very notion of method draws out the positive senex working behind the scenes of Hillman's thought. When well carried out, the outcome of the archetypal approach will always be *senex-et-puer*—on at least two levels: a unique, timely expression of timeless, universal principles; and an imaginative, poetically engaging insight that grows out of a sustained, thorough circumambulation of a theme.

Hillman's perceived need to approach matters from the puer side was occasioned by dominant senex structures, both within and beyond psychology. His entry into this topic coincided with the counter-cultural movement, which may have had its quintessential expression in America but was spreading around the world and inviting new values and visions of reality—its messages as loud and colorful as its music. He begins this early paper with a vivid description of the polarization between "age and youth"—in demographics, in family life, in politics, even in theology (2005, pp. 31-32). Yet despite the invitation to new thought, Hillman could see that a reactionary rejection of the old truths could be as unworkable as succumbing to mind-numbing traditionalism. Just as the senex structures had to be loosened, the puer impulse had to be understood and tempered. Even the humanistic and transpersonal psychology movements that began at the time struck Hillman as too one-sidedly optimistic, progressive, and spiritually infused. Too puer. Everyone was intent on climbing the peaks, while the vales were being left behind. In a sense, archetypal psychology emerged as a *counter*, counter-cultural reading of what the psyche needed—not simply a break with the past, but a reimagining of it. Even more critically, in revealing the mythic repetitions in the so-called facts of history, in culture and the arts, archetypal psychology was beginning to collapse the barrier between psyche and world. To psyche it brought phenomena and flesh; to world it brought animation.

Finally, senex and puer seem to pervade the very machinations of psychological life. Hillman suggests that "the puer personifies the moist spark within any complex or attitude. . . the call of a thing to the perfection of itself" (2005, p. 54) just as he describes "the structure and principles by which a complex endures" as "senex phenomena" (p. 274). Via such understandings he argues, "this specific archetype will be involved in the process character of any complex" (p. 36). For Hillman then, it's the embrace of the puer that opens up the teleological process Jung had earlier located as a creative potential within any complex. As noted above, "Every situation is headed somewhere" (2005, p. 106). And it's the senex, at least the negative senex, devoid of any puer inspiration, that prevents psychic movement and new understandings.

To the Essence

Let's, for a moment, go back to Jung. Hillman's image-centered conclusion to his first book, *Emotion* (1960) echoes Jung's famous insight at the heart of his "Confrontation with the Unconscious." In declaring that the ability to turn emotions into images allowed the transformation of the psyche, Jung set out the main means by which his psychology would bring conscious and unconscious into dialogue and eventual union. This is the symbolic life at the core of individuation; symbols and images bridge the upper and lower realms of being. Hillman largely stuck to the latter term because images and the contextual complexity they carry don't succumb to analytical interpretation in the same way that symbols do. Instead they invite other more subtle modes of thought and feeling, preserving the shaded complexity of the depths. Often an image will come to us—and we're used to thinking of them in this way—like a pre-packaged, meaning-laden gift from the psyche. But most of the time an image must be nursed into its imagistic substance—its significance—through deliberate tending. The centaur at the end of the book *Emotion* only *becomes* an image of significance in the context of the topic when Hillman expounds on its metaphoric potential: connecting the nature of emotion to the animal beneath or within us; relaying the creature's capacity to capture wild bulls and teach music. Also, in finding the fitting idea—"that wilder emotion can be tamed by conscious emotion"—the image finds a deeper resonance. Often idea and image will feed off of one another, yet an image also needs a kind of love to nurture it into fullness. Hillman's essay, "The Thought of the Heart" is the quintessential illustration of this understanding, where mind and heart converge on a soul terrain of imagistic possibility. He describes this as an "intelligence (that) takes places by means of images which are a third possibility between mind and world . . . a simultaneous knowing and loving by means of imagining" (1981, p. 7).

The very goal of archetypal psychology as Hillman conceived it is the cultivation of the imagination. What he came to call "a poetic basis of mind" (1997, pp. 14ff.) constitutes both the point of departure and the aim of the archetypal project. It "starts neither in the physiology of the brain, the structure of language, the organization of society, nor analysis of behavior, but in the processes of the imagination," acknowledging "the inherent relation between psychology and the cultural imagination" (p. 19). And it rests on the attempt "to realize the poetic basis of mind in actuality . . . when the environment is recognized as imagistic, then each person reacts to it in a more psychological manner" (p. 57). Early on he had used the term "imaginal ego" to describe the desired outcome of Jungian analysis (1972, pp. 183ff.)—a dedicated and lengthy interiorizing process. For *if,* as he writes, "an image always seems more profound (archetypal), more powerful (potential), and more beautiful (theophanic) than the comprehension of it" (1997, p. 18), *then* that profundity, power, and beauty (or sometimes dishevelment) will very much depend on our carefully cultivated capacity to sense and host these qualities. Soul requires *care*, as Thomas Moore advised us (1992). And if soul is a perspective not a substance, as Hillman argued at the start of *Re-Visioning Psychology*, then it's our ways of knowing, understanding, and sensing that require the tending. "Soul" and "imagination," the two primary terms in archetypal psychology, are in this way drawn together in Hillman's psychology of perspective, designating both the desired outcome and the path along which the process proceeds. As he wrote, "Soul-making is imagining" (1997, p. 36).

As indicated above, there's an unnamed ingredient at the heart of this approach. What Jung and Hillman shared in common was an exceptional phenomenological sense and eye for particulars. Their powers of entering and describing lived experience and the world they inhabited occupies the immediate background of their facility with symbols (Jung) and images (Hillman). Whereas it was Hillman that took the pagan polytheistic path as a means to push away from the monotheistic elements of Jung's view, both were polytheistic in their dexterity of imagination and metaphoric range. This, in particular, is what allows Hillman to employ his "method" so effectively. Sticking to the image—called "the golden rule of archetypal psychology's method" (1997, p. 18) often also means sticking to the topic: deepening, expanding, amplifying the point, increasing comprehension so that there's more room to digest what life presents. This is what the psyche loves, and it becomes the basis of seeing through. Or to bring the two actions together in a different way, sticking to the topic means sticking to the topic's imaginal possibilities. The process often erodes well-trodden paths and even shatters preconceptions.

And therein lies the genius of James Hillman. He could take an event, a motif, or some other slice of life and keep turning it until all kinds of soul-nurturing or iconoclastic insights issued forth. From friendship to betrayal, bugs to horses, and pornography to marriage, he took islands of understanding and turned them into archipelagos of deep reflection. Not explanation, often not even knowledge in the conventional sense, but all kinds of compelling ways for something to roam in the imagination. A deep polytheism of ideas and perspectives is what allowed him to do this. This recessed, unnamed polytheistic habit of mind is what really keeps the macro polytheism of archetypal psychology vital and viable, preventing it from falling into formula and stasis. This element of Hillman's approach is, in many ways, more foundational than the overt references to the gods. It is, at the end of the day, what allows his method to work. As much as a process to follow, Hillman's method is a call to complexity and nuance.

We thus come to the realization that whereas archetypal psychology may indeed have a method, it's not one that's easily extracted from the originator's work, nor can it be applied following an intellectual crash-course. It isn't just taken up; it must be lived into. For the method itself involves shifts in psychological perspective: from explanation to amplification; from understanding to imagining; from systematic comprehension to circumstantial insight. For those already attuned to Jung's psychology, Hillman's approach shifts the gravity of concern: from psychic contents to modes of perception; from clinical and conceptual language to mythic and poetic expression; from the interiority of soul to the *anima mundi*. Most of all, the archetypal method involves the constant reversion of psychological theory to mythic, archetypal configurations. It inverts day-world and ego concerns, placing our awareness in constant contact with the depths, ruled by the gods.

References

Hillman, J. (1960). *Emotion*. Evanston, IL: Northwestern University Press.

Hillman, J. (1972). *The myth of analysis*. Evanston, IL: Northwestern University Press.

Hillman, J. (1975). *Re-visioning psychology*. New York, NY: Harper & Row.

Hillman, J. (Ed.). (1979). *Puer papers*. Dallas, TX: Spring Publications.

Hillman, J. (1981). *The thought of the heart and the soul of the world*. Dallas, TX: Spring Publications.

Hillman, J. (1996). *The soul's code: In search of character and calling.* New York, NY: Random House.

Hillman, J. (1997). *Archetypal psychology: A brief account.* Woodstock, CT: Spring Publications.

Hillman, J. (2005). *Senex & puer.* G. Slater (Ed.), *Uniform edition of the writings of James Hillman* (Vol. 3). Putnam, CT: Spring.

Jung, C. G. (1960). *The structure and dynamics of the psyche.* CW, Vol. 8. London, UK: Routledge & Kegan Paul.

Moore, T. (1982). *Care of the soul.* New York, NY: HarperPerennial.

Russell, D. (2013). *The life and ideas of James Hillman: Volume I, The making of a psychologist.* New York, NY: Helios Press.

Slater, G. (2000). Archetypal fundamentalism in the twenty-first century. In D. Slattery and L. Corbett (Eds.). *Psychology at the threshold.* Carpinteria, CA: Pacifica Graduate Institute Publications.

HILLMAN AND FREIRE:
INTELLECTUAL ACCOMPANIMENT BY
TWO FATHERS

Mary Watkins

Introduction

Accompaniment, *acompañamiento,* used in the Latin American context comes from *compañero* or friend, and from the Latin *ad cumis pan,* to break bread together. To accompany is to walk alongside one another, lightening the load of going the path alone. Intellectual accompaniment can be accomplished by the living and the dead, by one physically near and by one whom we have never physically met, through spoken dialogue and the quiet imaginal dialogue provoked by an intense encounter with written works.

When Camilo Ghorayeb invited me to pay tribute to Hillman's work in Campinas, I thought of São Paulo, that city where at the end of his life Paulo Freire was entrusted with administering the then largest public school system in the world. I knew that speaking here I could not keep Hillman and Freire apart, although they never met and never mentioned one another in their work. I could not keep them apart here because it is here in Brazil that they came together in my life in 1985 when I adopted my oldest daughter from Natal in the *Nordeste.*

My life has been graced by my experience of them as intellectual fathers: Jim through his books, mentorship, and friendship, and Paulo through my deep immersion in his writings. Often those surrounding each of these men found my deep passion for the other's work highly suspect. I trusted in my own sense that while each of their works presented itself as a completed world, that only together, backed up against one another, did I begin to get a sense of the totality of the task before us, as psychologically minded people concerned with the deep economic and social divides between people and the frightening lack of regard for our effects on the natural world that has come to imperil all earthly beings.

Freire and Hillman lived in quite different worlds. Their social locations had radical impact on their work, and its positioning during the 1950's-1970's. We can see this clearly by their very different experiences of exile. Freire was forced into a painful and prolonged political exile after imprisonment for his political commitments. Hillman engaged in a self-chosen exile from his country, stepping aside from the politics of the day—except that is from the politics at the Zurich Jung Institute, which eventually double-exiled him back to his home country. This second exile situated him back home in a way that wider politics began to matter to him. Only in the 1980's did Hillman undergo a reorientation that brought his own understandings closer to Freire's. In the last decades of their lives both were grappling with the effects of globalization on communities.

Paulo Freire (1921-1997) was born in Recife, in the northeast of Brazil, five years before Hillman was born in Atlantic City, New Jersey, son of a successful hotelier. Freire began his life in a solidly middle-class family, with an army sergeant father and a seamstress housewife mother. Repercussions from the Depression in the United States suddenly threw his family into poverty. Freire recalled that while sitting in his classroom as a young boy, unable to concentrate on his lessons due to hunger, he silently forged a commitment to work on issues of world hunger when he grew up. Indeed, he did address hunger, but it was hunger for a sense of voice and agency, hunger for understanding the world one has taken as inevitable and unchangeable, and hunger to seize the "vocation of humanization" in order to transform the world one lives in.

After an extremely brief period as a lawyer, he launched a lifelong work on a radical revision of educational practices, contextualizing them in the local historical and political circumstances of the students. His work was fed by the Christian socialism of the 1960's and 1970's that rejected excess greed and the exploitation that it feeds on. He began creating cultural and literacy circles in the 1950's in northeast Brazil. He linked the gaining of literacy with learning to decode the socioeconomic and political configurations of power that scaffold one's everyday life. The method he evolved of developing critical consciousness entailed literacy work in a group based on dialogical practices, led by a group leader called an "animator."

Participants were asked what generative words, words at the heart of their daily experience, they would like to learn to read and write. With each word the animator asks questions to bring from the group their knowledge about the lived context of the word. For instance, "water" is a crucial word for a region alternately devastated by droughts and floods, a region where water rights are controlled by forces outside of ordinary people's influence. Generative questions would seek to help the group pull together their knowledge of the situation they found themselves in: Who controls the water? What are the illnesses that come from tainted water? How does water become polluted? Was it always so? Did people used to have access to more clean water? If so, what changed? Initially, said Freire, we accept our daily reality as inevitable, natural, and normal. It is only by beginning to reflect on it in the company of others that we can begin to see how it is constructed. Often then we tend to blame ourselves or particular others for the way things are. With further questioning and dialogue, however, we can begin to see into the deeper societal arrangements that create our daily experience. It is only at this point that we can begin to imagine things otherwise, and we can exercise prophetic imagination with others to vision a more preferred reality toward which we can work in solidarity with others.

In 1961, he was asked to initiate a literacy program that would involve teaching five million people previously denied education by institutions of neocolonialism. As in the United States where it was also forbidden to teach slaves how to read and write, such deprivation was used in northeast Brazil to disempower the masses and make claims of their inferiority easier. Such claims then rationalized abuses of laborers, as they do in the United States. Many were consigned to conditions of poverty, malnutrition, and illness in order that a few in power could profit.

In 1962 he directed a project where 300 rural farmworkers were taught to read and write in 45 days. In 1963 President Goulart invited Freire to rethink Brazil's approach to literacy and to coordinate the National Literacy Plan. Freire and his colleagues set up 200,000 cultural circles to host the emergence into literacy of two million Brazilians. A coup d'état replaced Goulart with a repressive military government. Shortly after the coup, Freire was imprisoned for 70 days, and was called an "international subversive," a "traitor to Christ and the Brazilian people," and was accused of trying to make Brazil a Bolshevik country (Gadotti, 1994, p. 35).

While in prison Freire grasped more deeply the essential connections between education and politics. The landowners had understood that through education the peasants would become aware of their social situation and begin to organize to improve their situation (Gadotti, 1994). He was exiled and moved his family briefly to Bolivia, where a coup led to his working in Chile on issues of agrarian reform, organizing peasants and small farmers, and consulting on literacy issues. He relished studying his method in another context, always claiming that a particular locale had to develop its own generative words and readers. During his time in Chile he was able to complete at age 47 *Pedagogy of the Oppressed,* first published in 1968, translated into dozens of languages, while being banned in most Latin American countries as well as the Iberian Peninsula during the years of his exile. His method has affected critical dialogical practice on all continents.

In my remarks today I want to draw attention to that fertile crescent of ideas that grow where the independent springs of Hillman and Freire's works co-mingle. As we face into the gathering storm of globalization's rapacious desires, we need both a psychology of how the oppressed can transform the situations they are born into and a psychology of how what Hillman called "white consciousness" can make a jailbreak from the "tiny cell" of the ego that has predisposed it to see the world as dead and lifeless. While Freire borrowed on Erich Fromm's work to describe the necrophilic character of oppressor consciousness, Hillman grappled with this mode of being at close range. From his own early adult experience, he came to be very aware of how white consciousness can ignore the difficulties of the world, choosing instead only the psychic interior for its engagement.

I first encountered Hillman's work when I was 22, and Freire's when I was 34.[1] In both cases I had a sense of being taken under the wing of a work, a work in both cases that I would devote years of my life to. In my late forties I began an essay comparing and contrasting their thought: "'Seeing Through' and 'Critical Consciousness': A Conversation between the Work of Hillman and Freire." It is only since Jim's death and upon your invitation that I have felt the freedom to

---

[1] I met Hillman first when reading *Suicide and the Soul* (1964/1997) a book recommended to me by my Jungian analyst when I was 22 in the wake of my discovering a woman patient at the hospital I was working in trying to kill herself. In 1973 I went to Zurich to study at the Jung Institute and hoped to approach Hillman to become my analyst. Only when I arrived in Zurich did I find that he had returned to Yale University for the fall, where he had first delivered the Terry Lectures in 1972. These lectures were soon to become *Re-Visioning Psychology* (1975a). In January 1974 he returned to Zurich and gave the lectures at the Jung Institute. The lecture hall was brimming with listeners and there was an unusual stillness and concerted concentration in the hall as he delivered these talks. At the time we could have only mis-named why. In retrospect, it was a beginning moment of the archetypal psychology movement, a movement that stirred and challenged the Jungian community and that was to provide needed critique and extension to depth psychology more generally.

Ten years later in 1984, working as a clinical psychologist, I was on the verge of becoming an adoptive mother to a baby daughter from northeast Brazil. My "pregnancy" was not the growing of a usual seed. My hunger was not for strange food combinations, but for everything "Nordeste": northeast Brazilian music, poetry, politics, and history. In this feasting I met the work of Paulo Freire through reading *Pedagogy of the Oppressed* (1968/2000), a work that has sparked movements for liberation throughout the world.

return to this essay. Thank you for this invitation.

Despite Freire and Hillman's many differences in life experiences and emphases in their work, they shared several core ideas and orientations: the difference between ideas and ideologies, the work of seeing-through ideas or critical consciousness, the relationship between reflection and action, a suspicion of dualities and a desire to overcome the contradictions they impose, the critical role of the imagination in human life, and our interdependence with one another and with nature.

Seeing Through and Critical Consciousness

How different Freire and Hillman's processes of developing consciousness were! Freire always worked with people in groups, believing that this empowered them to begin to think together about their shared situation; Hillman worked for decades in the dyadic arrangement of therapy, until he chose to abandon therapy, assessing that it was often part of the problem for the Euro-American person. Then he too often moved to the group, first in men's gatherings with poet Robert Bly, and then in classroom encounters that grew to be highly dialogical at Pacifica Graduate Institute and other places. He would later say that if groups were not sources of increasing consciousness, we would not find the right of assembly denied when a single point of view is trying to gain ascendancy.

At the heart of their work was what Hillman called "seeing-through," and what Freire called "conscientization" or the development of critical consciousness. Both sought to denaturalize the taken-for-granted, to reject the lies in many dominant narratives, and to seek knowledge that has been marginalized and even disappeared.

Ideas and Ideologies

Both men's stated goals—soul-making for Hillman and

humanization for Freire—are foundationally dependent on working with and through ideas. Whereas Hillman initially focused on seeing-through psychological material and personality issues, through the 1980's he moved to seeing-through societal and ecological conditions, much as Freire had already been doing.

Hillman asserted that "soul-making takes place as much through ideation as in personal relationships or meditation" (1975a, p. 115). Indeed, his opus is a staggering gift that teaches us at every turn how to live in relationship with ideas: loving them, critiquing them, turning them, seeing-through them, wrestling with them, being devoted to them, being animated by them, sacrificing to them, and caring for them. Hillman wrote, "We are always in the embrace of an idea," and our "wrestling with [them] is a sacred struggle" (p. 121).

Freire saw ideas as the scaffolding of our societal structures, and as the *prima materia* with which we transform our world. For both men, it is our unreflected identification with and possession by ideas, which condemns us to mindlessly repeat the past and support the destructive status quo configurations of the present. Hillman saw this work as "dethroning the dominant fantasy ruling our view of the world" (1975a, p. 41). Ideas need to be seen through, reflected upon, taken up as things that are created and which can be transformed. Hillman warned that psyche without ideas turns to ideologies. "Psychologizing sees through what is taught; it is a learning beyond any teaching" (p. 133).

For Freire, the radical is one who can think critically. He is able to doubt, to suspend circles of certainties within which reality is imprisoned. "He is not afraid to confront, to listen, to see the world unveiled" (1968/2000, p. 24). Such bold sight has the goal of transforming the pernicious aspects of reality in concert with others.

When ideas are unworked, the reality they spawn is experienced as natural or inevitable. The experiencer is, in turn, a passive victim. "The soul seems to suffer," said Hillman, "when its inward eye is occluded, a victim of overwhelming events" (1975a, p. 123). Psyche desires vision. "Ideas," said Hillman, "are the nodes that make possible our ability to see through events into their patterns" (p.

121), "dethroning the dominant fantasy ruling our view of the world" (p. 41).

It is the posing of questions for Freire, questions that lead people to reflect on the given, that allow the generative ideas of a situation to surface, and to be reflected upon. For Freire the process of grasping the ideas that structure everyday experience allows us to partake of a process of humanization, which he saw as our ontological vocation. It is this seeing-through that liberates us to create with ideas, rather than only be a victim of them. Hillman and Freire agreed that seeing-through is never accomplished once and for all, but is a continual process. Freire warned that without this ongoing reflection, oppression reoccurs, even if it is the former victims who now perpetrate it, having simply identified with the consciousness of their former oppressors.

The kind of education that both men would seek is education that both exposes ideas and allows us to envision by means of them. The liberation of ideas from the blindness of ideology is a key value for both thinkers. Then, said Hillman, "Ideas are ways of seeing and knowing, or knowing by means of insighting. Ideas allow us to envision and by means of vision we can know" (1975a, p. 121).

Reflection and Action

For both men, "action and idea are not inherent enemies, and," as Hillman asserted, "they should not be paired as a contrast" (1975a, p. 116). Hillman saw reflection as an activity and "action as always enact[ing] an idea" (p. 116). He spoke of our needing "to bring soul into action, and action into soul by means of psychologizing" (p. 117). Ideas change practice, he said. "When an insight or idea has sunk in, practice invisibly changes. The idea has opened the eye of the soul. By seeing differently, we do differently" (p. 122). Given Hillman's commitment to ideas and his relative lack of interest in method and practice, it is important to underscore his clarity about this. Freire also stressed the necessity to move between action and reflection, and thus not to split into either an activism devoid of reflection or a kind of reflection that degenerates into mere "verbalism."

Freire, like Hillman, was committed to overcoming contradictions, not being caught in them. He sought to overcome identification with either pole of the duality of oppressor and oppressed. He knew how easily those who have been subjected to oppression can nevertheless identify with the oppressor and breed more oppression when they have seized power. "Man in the process of liberation" was the alternative for Freire to the oppressor-oppressed duality.

The Problematizing and Relativizing of the "Modern Ego"

Hillman did not focus thematically, as Freire did, on colonialism, coloniality, or the effects of colonialism on the psyche. His work, however, can be read as a gradual attempt to problematize—using Freire's language—aspects of oppressor consciousness, certain forms of the Western or Euro-American ego. As early as 1972 in *The Myth of Analysis* we can begin to track his suspicion of the Western ego, his characterizing it as the most unconscious aspect of a person. He saw its heroic proclivities, and often characterized it as "the conquering ego" or "the imperial ego." Hillman, a son of the First World, was beginning to work his way out of psychoanalysis' lauding of the ego. His critique unfolded like a gathering storm that burst upon first Jungian psychology's adoration of the Self and the individuation process, and then upon a host of embedded assumptions with depth psychology generally about the function of the ego.

As others since have realized how colonial discourse became embedded in the psychoanalytic project, Hillman was listening to the imperialism in the way that Freud characterized the task of the ego: "To strengthen the ego, to make it more independent of the super-ego, to widen its field of perception and enlarge its organization so that it can appropriate fresh portions of the id, where id was there shall ego be. It is a work of culture" (Freud, 1964, pp. 99-100). Hillman read as

"Romanizing" Freud's metaphorical image of the ego as draining sea-marshes to reclaim land.

In *Myth of Analysis* (1972) Hillman spoke of the ascension of the psyche to the head in 18th century philosophy and saw this as a beginning "of the contemporary fantasy of a 'strong ego.'" This new ego, he said,

> appeared in fears of softness and the influence of Venus, in the strengthenings through iron, in the search in the brain for the essence of personality, in the notion of madness as a disorder of brain mechanisms and breakdown of control, in the doctrines of racial and male superiority, in the peculiar rationale of managed torture as therapy. . . .
>
> Most of the language of psychology developed within the same context which saw the rise of the modern ego. This language reflects its context, a psyche identified with the head and without eros, an "empire" of the hard, strong, materialized ego. Thus the descriptions and the judgments in this language cannot help but reflect the point of view of this structure of consciousness, to which we are so habituated that we have come to call it "ego." Each of us accepts this collective structure so unthinkingly, so irrevocably, that each believes it to be his very own unique and private "I." (1972, pp. 153-154)

Hillman saw that the identification with the idea of centered rule by will and reason co-constellates an unconscious marked by disintegration and fragmentation. He wants us to see these as styles of consciousness: the center and the periphery, each with their own values, strengths, and patterns of fantasy.

He was looking at how divisions in the self, such as in schizophrenia, were beginning to end the "rule of reason" (1975a, p. 25). Cases of multiple personality, he said, confirmed

> the multiplicity of the individual at a time when the same phenomenon was beginning to appear in the culture in general.

> Through this multiple schizoid perspective we saw a world no
> longer held together by reason, no *longer held and centered at
> all.* Instead: disordering spontaneity, relativity, discontinuities,
> aharmonies, an overpopulation of spirits and living soul
> images—the return of archetypal persons. (p. 25)

He saw central command losing control as individuality of the
parts assert themselves against central authority. He was aware that this
happens also in grassroot movements, but in this period he was
doggedly concerned with the psychic dynamics.

Hillman railed against what he understood as ideologies of
development that were consistent with the imperial ego. "The model of
thinking is nineteenth-century," he said, "a primitive Darwinism of
evolution, dominant over recessive; a psychological imperialism,
colonizing the unconscious or the id with a reality-coping ego
consciousness" (1972, p. 184). Hillman said, "We still tend to think of
'development' as a progressive march whose retreats are only for a
better leap forward. . . and which is modeled upon the hero's
opposition to an irrational imaginal world beyond his powers of
control" (p. 184). He understood that "the conceptual structure of
psychopathology ha[d] arisen parallel with the specific ego
development of the past century and a half" that he was describing (p.
184). A move to the imaginal ego involved removing oneself from the
path of development of the heroic ego, the ego of mastery and control,
of self-sufficiency, and individualistic achievement. "The imaginal
ego," he said, "is more discontinuous, now this and now that, guided as
much by the synchronistic present as by the causal past. . . . It includes
the downward turns, the depressions, recessions, and fallings-away
from awareness. Psychopathology has its place; it is necessary" (p. 184).
He wrote that the movement of the imaginal ego should be conceived
more as a circle than as a linear development.

During this same period Freire was also concerned with
development, but in his case it is the idea of development and progress
that was thrust on some societies by other societies. As liberation
theologians had also argued, such imposition actually caused

underdevelopment for many to support the presumed development for a few. Freire and others argued that each society should be free to undertake its own path of development.

In saying "modern ego" Hillman was not including the ego of those marginalized in society. He was describing the ego of people like himself in the West. The problems of passivity, fatalism, and over-accommodation to reality as received that Freire took up as characteristic of the ego of the peasants he was working with is nowhere to be found in Hillman.

In his essay "On Anima" Hillman turned the ego on its head, saying that it is not a king but a janitor, an instrument for day-to-day coping, and that "from the traditional psychology (of Neoplatonism), ego consciousness does not deserve the name of consciousness at all" (1991, p. 33). The myth of the hero, he said, is the myth of inflation. "The hero myth tells the tale of conquest and destruction, the tale of psychology's 'strong ego,' its fire and sword, as well as the career of its civilization, but it tells little of the culture of its consciousness" (p. 32). But, said Hillman, "the ego is not the whole psyche, only one member of a commune" (1975a, p. 31).

Psychic Polytheism and the Imaginal Ego

In the early 1970's, in the rather closed society of the Jung Institute in Zurich, the way that Hillman proposed an undoing of this psychic empire was by a turn from psychic monotheism to polytheism, a turn to the multiple psychic figures that animate what Jung called the mythopoetic function of the psyche. In "collapsing the rule of the old ego," Hillman was aware that the "abandonment of psychological monotheism is radical indeed" (1972, p. 265).

In this period Hillman advocated for a radical change in the function of the ego, from a Romanizing ascendancy of an ever more powerful ego to an imaginal ego. This latter ego's function is far more humble. It is to host the multiplicity of the psyche through active imagination and reflection through archetypal lenses. While almost wholly inner oriented, this period in Hillman's work was crucial to his dethroning of the ego, and his own intimate witness of the vibrant wilds of imagination that are then accessible, not only as feared inbreaks of psychic symptoms, but as regions with interest of their own, and which offer refreshment and revitalization to the parched and retired leaders of Roman legions.

In 1972 Hillman saw that "fantasies are incompatible with my usual ego, and because they are uncontrollable and 'fantastic'—that is, away from the relation to ego reality—we feel them alien. . . . *our fantasies are alien because they are not ours*" (1972, p. 182). He understood that "the ego expands. . . at the cost of childhood's godlike, dimmer light of wonder, of imagination, and the symbolic, natural mind. Creativity through the ego is necessary and yet it is a theft, a sin, a Luciferian fall" (p. 45).

A few years later in *Re-Visioning Psychology,* Hillman proclaimed with an air of certainty, "Personifying is the soul's answer to egocentricity" (1975a, p. 32). During this period he focused on the autonomy of the psyche, the capacity of the psyche to generate fantasy, to see in terms of psychic figures. His project was a decentering of the psyche through a relativizing of the ego, and an emphasizing that consciousness resides in each psychic figure and landscape, not only in the ego. In *The Dream and the Underworld* he maintained that the "first move in teaching ego how to dream is to teach it about itself, that it too is an image," to teach it how to move in the dark (1975b, p. 102).

In doing so he was clear that he was following Jung's lead in trying to develop a new kind of ego consciousness through "taking the dream ego with utter seriousness and by training consciousness to think symbolically or psychologically" (1972, p. 183). He said,

> Jung thus seemed to make war on merely rational thinking, and thus he relegated the will to a smaller role. These powers of the soul, and the ego attitudes derived from them, prevented awareness of another sort. He had found that therapy in depth depended upon just this other sort of ego consciousness, an imaginal awareness that leads to another sort of ego attitude.

(p. 183)

While Hillman saw Jung as "pointing beyond the ego concept of the nineteenth century with its emphasis upon head, will, and reason," he believed that analytical psychology had not worked "out a concept of the ego corresponding with Jung's" intuition, "which puts such stress on imaginal consciousness—dream, vision, fantasy—and on a life-style (the symbolic life) in which the ego lives and behaves primarily in terms of imaginal consciousness. The old concept of ego development is anachronistically retained" (1972, pp. 183-184). For this reason Hillman focused on what he called the "imaginal ego," using Henry Corbin's sense of the word "imaginal," pointing to an altogether different realm of the real, not the "imaginary." He proposed that the imaginal ego is that part of the ego complex that can engage in imaginal reality. This shift to an imaginal ego, Hillman suggested, would allow us to be in contact with what can heal us, a realm always otherwise beyond the threshold of the heroic ego (1972). He asks us to question our own location in the ego and to bare ourselves to encounters with those standpoints far from the center of ego consciousness.[2]

In *Myth of Analysis* in 1972, Hillman was conserving the individualistic self, even as he struggled against the ego. The attention is given to what arises within oneself. The gaze is inward, to the margins of consciousness, and down into the psychic depths. He saw that we are living in a sliver of ourselves, suffering an amputation of consciousness, splitting us off from libidinal springs of the imaginal. But there is no link to the larger world within which such an ego resides, no link yet made between the psychic and the social depths.

---

[2] In commenting on Hillman's idea of the imaginal ego, volume editor Thomas Moore (1991) says in *A Blue Fire* that Hillman's move toward the poetic basis of mind, moves consciousness away from heroics to "a more receptive and malleable posture." "A relaxed ego that honors the many offers considerable rewards. We find vitality in tension, learn from paradox, gather wisdom by straddling ambivalence, and gain confidence in trusting the confusion that naturally arises from multiplicity" (p. 38).

White Consciousness

In his essay "Notes on White Supremacy," Hillman (1986) took up the white supremacy of the Northern European and American psyche that sees whiteness as superior to darkness. He tracked how this whiteness is likened both to superiority and with the supposed purity and innocence of the child. He understood how "the convention informing geographical discoveries and the expansion of white consciousness over Africa. . . informs psychic geography, the topological language used by Freud for 'the unconscious' as a place below, different, timeless, primordial, libidinal and separated from consciousness" (p. 45). This psychic geography "recapitulates," he said, "what white reporters centuries earlier said about west Africa" (p. 45). Then he made a bold claim that I would like to underscore:

> It is this unconscious white consciousness that is the proper object of depth psychology, depth come home to roost, out of Africa; depth in Freud's sense of the omnipotence fantasy and Jung's sense of shadow, ever present and always mine, the very me I am now, imagining myself eternal and unblamed. . . . And so the entire modern psychological effort to raise consciousness, and the ego drafted to enact the endeavor, is one more manifestation of whiteness, perpetuating the very fault it would resolve. The project can never succeed since the unconscious it would redeem lies in the instrument of its intent, in the eye of its light. (1986, p. 46)

Hillman described the historical path to white consciousness:

> As modern psychology recognized this double delusion—that its selective consciousness does not really require another and that this consciousness really does refer to another—it had to divide the mind. It had to invent the unconscious in order to remind consciousness that it could never be as white as it wishes. The "discovery" of the "unconscious" came as a late

stage of modernism, indicating its decline by turning its projective roots back onto itself. The "discovery" was actually a self-discovery, a backhanded welcoming of reflective consciousness's own delusional base, turning the delusion into irony and joke, a way to look back over its own shoulder, to reflect its own downfall, to become "post." The ego that feels itself as weak attempts to assert more and more control of what is alien. (pp. 54-55)

Hillman went on to describe the psychic orientation of white consciousness as one whereby one believes one is seeing others, but is only seeing oneself. Further, one is unaware that one is being seen, by human others and even other-than-human others, including night itself. White consciousness has to "discover" otherness; it has to realize that it is an infinitesimally small island in comparison to all that is around, above, and below it. White consciousness can travel far abroad without realizing what it contributes to what it falsely pronounced that it "discovers." Its racism and the unconsciousness of its missionary zeal go unquestioned, perpetuating harm where it only sees the "gift" of its own whiteness.

> The alchemical opus takes place *in vivo* as well as *in vitro*. There is the vessel of the world which too is psyche. Which too has eyes. . . . This yielding to the image-pregnant materiality of the world is how I would today define "psychic consciousness." The world does not need the missionary; it is already converted, enlightened with its own opalescence. . . . Today we will say psychic consciousness is not creative but created, and we the world's creatures. All we need to do is to open our eyes to its eyes. (1986, p. 52)

Until we open our eyes and see others looking at us, the world is cast as dead and we treat it as such: the people, the animals, the streams, the air, the mountains.

Here Hillman and Freire's work back up into one another, each requiring the other's insights into the mindsets that both manufacture and are affected by oppression and exploitation. From the trajectory of his own depth psychological work, Hillman began to describe the roots of what Freire called "oppressor consciousness." Freire followed Erich Fromm's lead in distinguishing biophilic from necrophilic consciousness, and associated oppressor consciousness with the latter. "And the more the oppressors control the oppressed," said Freire (1968/2000), "the more they change them into apparently inanimate 'things.' This tendency of the oppressor consciousness to 'in-animate' everything and everyone it encounters, in its eagerness to possess, unquestionably corresponds to a tendency to sadism" (p. 45).

Hillman began to experience the eyes of others, saying "They've got eyes on me; I am their referent, their text. 'I' have fallen out of my mind, out of the twentieth century, no place to hide and everywhere to go" (1986, p. 42). In *Myth of Analysis* in 1972 he described how "the 'strong' ego, that first aim of psychotherapy, is thus opposed to and then overwhelmed by the numinous Wholly Other" (p. 185). There he was referring to the imaginal other. In 1986, 14 years later, the others who were seeing him were human, animal, and earth others, in addition to imaginal others.

Jailbreak: Ensouling the Ego

White consciousness walls itself in,[3] and is distressed that what it finds is always dead. Our failure to see the life in things "imprison[s] us," said Hillman, "in that tight little cell of the ego" (1998, p. 103). This is indeed a problem for those who inhabit such consciousness, and it is a problem for all that finds itself deanimated and exploited as though dead already. From one perspective, Hillman's work is a committed opus to the ongoing work of jailbreak, a form of psychic decolonization of oppressor consciousness.

First, he worked his way out of the imperial and colonizing ego

---

[3] "Having walled itself in, it blames it on the wall" (Hillman, 1986, p. 54).

by turning his attention to the multiplicities of psychic life, to its imaginal figures. Living in Zurich, away from his own native politics in the U.S., Hillman turned to the interior world to work within. In the 1980's, now living back in the U.S., he began to understand the enclosed psychic universe that he had participated in. In a 1994 essay, "Psychology, Self, and Community," he confessed: "I stayed there [in Zurich] until unable to differentiate individuation from alienation" (1994/2006, p. 109). He clarified that the locus of the soul was not and had never been internal to the person, but that rather the person is *in* soul. The person is ensouled, along with each and every other: human and other than human. It came out awkwardly at first, by his noticing toasters and bad chairs. Later he saw sparks of life in animals, taking note of their eachness and particularity. He found he had to abandon the practice of psychotherapy in order to facilitate his own jailbreak from the tiny tight cell of the ego, to release his noticing into the wider world. He was seeking to awaken from what he called the anesthesia of "the subjectivism of psychotherapy, as if the end of the world were an 'inner problem'" (1998, p. 125).

In his 1982 essay "*Anima Mundi*: The Return of the Soul to the World," he leveled a corrective critique against the subjectivisitic and narcissistically oriented interpretive practices of depth psychology:

> To interpret the world's things as if they were our dreams deprives the world of its dreams, its complaint. Although this may have been a step toward recognizing the interiority of things, it finally fails because of the identification of interiority with only human subjective experience. (1998, p. 80)

He continued,

> Having divided psychic reality from hard or external reality, psychology elaborates various theories to connect the two orders together, since the division is worrisome indeed. It means that psychic reality is conceived to be neither public, objective, nor physical, while external reality, the sum of

existing material objects and conditions, is conceived to be utterly devoid of soul. As the soul is without world, so the world is without soul. (1998, p. 95)

Freire was quite clear that subjectivity should not be divorced from objectivity, from the concrete realities in which our lives unfold. Hillman came to understand the importance of the objective sociocultural context much later, but when he did, he was clear that it had been a blind spot in the Jungian and archetypal psychologies he had spent so many years working within. Once he understood that soul is in the world, and that we are in the soul, his vision turned outward. The pathology he had tracked so carefully on the interior was now clearly in the world, in our systems, our ideologies, and our relationships.

Imagination and Annunciation

Hillman and Freire meet again in underscoring the importance of imagination. Seeing-through and the development of critical consciousness are intimately related to the capacity to imagine. Hillman said: "Ideas allow us to envision and by means of vision we can know" (1975a, p. 120).

As one develops a critical consciousness of a particular situation, one understands how the situation has been constructed, created. One can denounce the destructive aspects. The work does not stop, however, with denunciation. Denunciation opens the path for what Freire called annunciation, sometimes treated as prophetic imagination. Freire activates creative imagination by recognizing the possibility for creation inherent in all impasses. In his language, "limit situations," where we at first seem unable to imagine how things can be otherwise, are the very location where the most intense experiences of prophetic imagination can occur.

For each, there is a preparation for imagining through ideas and through a realignment of the self. Given their difference in social location, however, the preparation is different. For the oppressed, conscientization empowers the self. One moves from a sense of being a victim of history with an attendant sense of pervasive fatalism and helplessness to a sense of oneself as able to understand and analyze in concert with others. For Hillman, who was working through and out of what he called white consciousness, the ego must relinquish its propensity to overcontrol and dominate, its tendency to attribute what is to itself. The ego must undergo a transformation in which it is humbled and finds itself in a world not of its own making. The ego, chastened and reduced from its hubris and self-enclosure, can now attend to what is unfolding, to all that is autonomous. Hillman learned this first in the realm of the imagination, and thus equated this different kind of non-heroic ego to what he called an imaginal ego.

Reading these two men side-by-side, we experience a kind of transcendent function. While Freire emphasized imagination as an empowering act that is preliminary to creating and acting in the world, Hillman emphasized the way in which imagining is a gateway for our presence to what is created beyond us by the objective psyche. If we are truly attentive to the imaginal, I would argue, we find that the objective and the subjective merge. The social, political, and economic bleed into images, just as the wild abandon of images that have yet to be embodied break out into the world to invent the new and the deeply desired.

Arriving at the Commons

Today we face the task of alterglobalization, of creating global social movements that reject economic and neoliberal globalization while working to protect human rights, indigenous rights, and climate and environmental well-being. When I imagine scholar-activists meeting at this global commons, Hillman is coming from the North and Freire from the South. In their conversation, the *socius* and the psyche converge, granting us clearer vision for our work ahead.

Once Hillman was clear that the soul is surrounding us, his attention, which he termed *notitia*, turned outwards to meet it. In 1988 he returned to Alfred Adler's work in his essay "Power and *Gemeinschaftsgefühl*." Hillman said that in Jung we do not have "a social feeling, fellow feeling, community concern, *Gemeinschaftsgefühl*" (p. 99). "Freud and Jung had located depth in only one place. They did not grasp the true depth in the 'out there,' in the *Gemeinschaftsgefühl*" (p. 99). He critiqued Freud and Jung for not imagining, he said,

> far enough, fundamentally enough, into the disorder of the world of concrete things, government institutions, commercial practices—the physical, political, and economic unconscious—those symptoms and those pathologies. Freud and Jung and their schools internalize the world and believe it can be dealt with mainly in an internalized fashion.[4] Clean up your own neurosis and that will clean up the world. . . .
>
> I think an Adlerian must see things very differently. If the out there is a primary place of the unconscious, then the ways of the world must be tackled directly. Hence, we understand Adler's interest in teachers and tailors and in the socialist movement. Politics is psychology: depth psychology is also depth sociology; to go truly deep is to go into the soul of the world. (p. 101)[5]

He embraced Adler's fellow feeling and renamed it "common" feeling, and then he extended it. Hillman said, "If we follow the ironic logic of *Gemeinschaftsgefühl* fully into community, community does not stop with human beings" (1988/2006, p. 104). Adler recognized what he called "the general interdependence of the cosmos from which

---

[4] This is less true of certain Freudian schools than of Jungian ones. See Ellen Danto, *Freud's Free Clinics: Psychoanalysis and Social Justice, 1918-1938* and Watkins & Shulman (2008), Chapter Four: Symptoms and Psychologies in Cultural Context, in *Toward Psychologies of Liberation*.

[5] Hillman continues, "Yes, power conflicts operate between parts of the psyche, Yes, there is an internal struggle to master and suppress. But let us not forget the clash of powers in the psychic depths of the world soul disguised as political, natural, social, and economic" (1988/2006, p. 101).

we cannot abstract ourselves completely!" (Adler, quoted in Hillman, 1988/2006, pp. 104-105). Hillman argued that we should not reduce the cosmos to society, to human beings only. He added "the rocks and the waters, the soil and the air, and all the material things made by the human community as well. . . " (p. 105).

When Hillman and Freire meet at the commons to share in the project of alterglobalization, they realize that they have each been involved in the work of psychic decolonization, Freire of those marginalized and Hillman of those who have found themselves inside the prison of what he called modern consciousness. Each confides how in their early thought they did not pay any attention to land, water, mountains, and animals. Freire at the end of his life was working on the Earth Charter, which is said to have been on his bedside table at his death. Hillman helped to launch the ecopsychology movement with his essay in Theodore Roszak, Mary Gomes, and Allen D. Canner's edited volume *Ecopsychology: Restoring the Earth, Healing the Mind* (1995). Hillman shares with Freire that he learned that the word "therapy" originally meant tending, caring for, giving attention to, in service of (1988/2006, p. 106), and that he came to understand the importance of "service to the soul of the world, a service that practices inferiority rather than overcomes it" (p. 106). He tells Freire how he turned to a therapy of the world, turning his eye to architecture, transit systems, schools, battlefields, the terrible love of war.

As he does in his essay about Adlerian psychology, he invokes the Commons in Thompson, Connecticut, a hundred yards from his home. Hillman riffed on the word "common": "as the village green in my New England hamlet was once a common for all bodies, human and nonhuman, to take part in common, care for in common, enjoy in common, common as ordinary, as common to all, this world so very common, so very dear, so much the source and the goal of our feeling" (1988/2006, p. 106).

What a trajectory from the imperial ego, to the commune of the psyche, to delight in the common—to the taking up difficulties-in-common! Hillman railed:

Herbicides, landfills, river pollution, strip mining, and other multinational agribusiness conglomerate horrors, even the litter in our streets begins not merely in the need and greed of industrialized consumerism. The way we treat the world out there begins in excluding it from the realm of soul, as if it were a great Cartesian corpse. (1988/2006, pp. 103-104)

I began this essay from that place in my own intimate life experience where the work of Hillman and Freire co-fathered me. We have arrived at the end of the essay, hopefully however, in seeing the need for the convergence of liberatory psychologies from the North and the South—not into a single proscriptive psychology that is ignorant of geographical and sociocultural differences—but into a sustained reflection on the common roots of our intersecting disorders. That imperial ego that has drained the resources of so many regions of the world, that has so crassly used the labor of millions, and practiced terror to sustain its untenable grasp, this imperial ego, Hillman showed, also starved itself. It gradually became so tightly contained in its cell, that it was removed from all sense of childhood wonder, encapsulated by a world it regarded as dead. It lost its vision and could only see its own backyard. It forgot that others also see; that their sight registers the effects of tyranny and terror, of kindness, compassion, and beauty.

In their own ways, both Freire and Hillman were revolutionaries. Psychiatrist and revolutionary Frantz Fanon in *Black Skins, White Masks* (1952/2008) called the middle-class "a closed society in which life has no taste, in which the air is tainted, in which ideas and men are corrupt. And I think that a man who takes a stand against this death is in a sense a revolutionary" (p. 225). Jim became this kind of revolutionary. He visited Civil War Battlefields, and spoke with bell hooks on racism in America. He could speak dialogically with students, and be the center of state occasions in Italy. He enjoyed the beauty in life, and had a soft fondness for animals. His opus, considered at this distance, constitutes a jailbreak from the imperial ego. Giving up the institutional politics of the Jungian world, abandoning psychotherapy as his practice, and returning to America from his self-imposed exile, he walked into a wider world that one sensed had an undeniable sweetness. At the very end of his life, he would frequently smile gently and wryly and announce that he was happy, that he felt truly loved. He seemed released, indeed, and in the sweet embrace of life.

References

Danto, E. (2007). *Freud's free clinics: Psychoanalysis and social justice, 1918-1938.* New York, NY: Columbia University Press.

Fanon, F. (2008). *Black skins, white masks.* New York, NY: Grove Press. (Original work published 1952)

Freire, P. (1992). *Pedagogy of hope: Reliving Pedagogy of the Oppressed.* New York, NY: Continuum.

Freire, P. (2000). *Pedagogy of the oppressed.* New York, NY: Bloomsbury Academic. (Original work published 1968)

Freud, S. (1964). *New introductory lectures on psycho-analysis.* New York, NY: W.W. Norton.

Gadotti, M. (1994). *Reading Paulo Freire.* Albany, NY: State University of New York Press.

Hillman, J. (1972). *The myth of analysis: Three essays in archetypal psychology.* Evanston, IL: Northwestern University Press.

Hillman, J. (1975a). *Re-visioning psychology.* New York, NY: Harper & Row.

Hillman, J. (1975b). *The dream and the underworld.* New York, NY: Harper & Row.

Hillman, J. (1986). Notes on white supremacy: Essaying an archetypal account of historical events. *Spring,* 1986, 29-58.

Hillman, J. (1997). *Suicide and the soul* (2nd ed.). Woodstock, CT: Spring Publications, Inc. (Original work published 1964)

Hillman, J. (1998). *The thought of the heart and the soul of the world.* Putnam, CT: Spring Publications.

Hillman, J. (2006). Power and Gemeinschaftsgefühl. In R. J. Leaver (Ed.), *City and soul: Uniform edition of the writings of James Hillman* (Vol. 2, pp. 96-107). Putnam, CT: Spring. (Original work published 1988)

Hillman, J. (2006). Psychology, self, and community. In R. Leaver (Ed.), *City and soul: Uniform edition of the writings of James Hillman* (Vol. 2, pp. 108-115). Putnam, CT: Spring. (Original work published 1994)

Moore, T. (Ed.). (1991). *A blue fire: Selected writings by James Hillman.* New York, NY: HarperPerennial.

Roszak, T., Gomes, M., and Canner, A. D. (Eds.). (1995). *Ecopsychology: Restoring the earth, healing the mind.* San Francisco, CA: Sierra Club Books.

Watkins, M. & Shulman, H. (2008). *Toward psychologies of liberation.* New York, NY: Palgrave Macmillan.

ABOUT THE AUTHORS

Stephen Aizenstat, Ph.D. is the Chancellor and Founding President of Pacifica Graduate Institute. He has explored the power of dreams through depth psychology and his own research for more than 35 years.

Gustavo Barcellos, M.A. is a Jungian analyst, a member of the Associação Junguiana do Brasil-AJB and the International Association for Analytical Psychology-IAAP, and editor of *Cadernos Junguianos*, AJB's journal. He is author of many books and articles in Brazil and abroad, who writes and teaches in the field of archetypal psychology. He holds a private practice in São Paulo, Brazil.

Edward Casey, Ph.D. is Distinguished Professor of Philosophy at SUNY, Stony Brook, and Distinguished Adjunct Faculty at the Pacifica Graduate Institute. He was recently elected president of the American Philosophical Association, Eastern Division, in 2009-2010. He is the author of ten books. His website is www.edwardscasey.com.

Lunalva Fiuza Chagas, M.A. is a psychologist and analyst member of the Brazilian Jungian Association (AJB). She is a member of the Institute of Analytical Psychology of Campinas (IPAC), of the International Association for Analytical Psychology, a guest professor in the specialization in Analytical Psychology of

Unicamp, and a teaching director at the Brazilian Jungian Association (AJB).

Camilo Francisco Ghorayeb is a clinical psychologist taking a master's degree in depth psychology with emphasis in Jungian and Archetypal studies at Pacifica Graduate Institute. He has also been working on projects and events with Pacifica Graduate Institute in Brazil.

Laurence Hillman, M.A. is a full-time professional astrologer and life and business coach. Laurence holds a B.A. in Architecture and Master's degrees in both Engineering Management and Business Administration. He has lectured internationally and conducted workshops at London's Globe Theatre (where he blended Shakespeare and Astrology), in Findhorn Scotland, and he is a regular lecturer at various Jung Societies across the United States. His website is www.lhillman.com.

Safron Rossi, Ph.D. is Associate Core Faculty in the Depth Psychology Jungian and Archetypal Studies MA/PhD program at Pacifica Graduate Institute, teaching courses on mythology and depth psychology. Safron is also Curator of Collections at Opus Archives & Research Center, home of the archival and manuscript collections of scholars including Joseph Campbell, James Hillman, and Marija Gimbutas. Her writing and scholarly studies focus on archetypal psychology, the western astrological tradition, goddess traditions, and feminist studies. Safron edited a volume in Joseph Campbell's *Collected Works* based on his Goddess mythology lectures titled *Goddesses: Mysteries of the Feminine Divine* (2013). She has published articles in Jungian and Archetypal journals and has contributed essays to various volumes including: *The Soul Does Not Specialize: Revaluing the Humanities and the Polyvalent Imagination*; and *Breaking the Plates: Fracturing Fictions and Archetypal Imaginings*.

Jennifer Leigh Selig, Ph.D. is core faculty and research coordinator at Pacifica Graduate Institute. She has collaborated with Dennis Patrick Slattery on two books *Reimagining Education: Essays on Reviving the Soul of Learning*, and *The Soul Does Not Specialize: Revaluing the Humanities and the Polyvalent Imagination*, and is the sole author of numerous essays and several books, including *Thinking Outside the Church: 110 Ways to Connect With Your Spiritual Nature*, and *Integration: Martin Luther King, Jr. and His (Unfinished) Therapy with the Soul of America*. Her website, including some of her essays and her photography, is www.jenniferleighselig.com.

Glen Slater, Ph.D., has studied and trained in religious studies and clinical psychology. For the past 16 years he has taught Jungian and archetypal psychology at Pacifica Graduate Institute. He edited and introduced the third volume of James Hillman's Uniform Edition, *Senex and Puer*, as well as a volume of essays by Pacifica faculty, *Varieties of Mythic Experience*, (with Dennis Patrick Slattery) and has contributed a number of essays to *Spring* journal and other Jungian publications.

Mary Watkins, Ph.D., is a core faculty member in the M.A./Ph.D. Depth Psychology Program at Pacifica Graduate Institute, Coordinator of its community and ecological fieldwork and research, and Co-Chair of its specialization in community psychology, liberation psychology, and ecopsychology. Her website, "Towards Psychologies of Liberation," is http://mary-watkins.net/.

www.ingramcontent.com/pod-product-compliance
Lightning Source LLC
Chambersburg PA
CBHW070804290326
41931CB00011BA/2132